DISCIPLINE

WITHOUT TEARS *Revised Edition*

*How to Reduce Conflict and
Establish Cooperation in the Classroom*

DISCIPLINE

WITHOUT TEARS *Revised Edition*

How to Reduce Conflict and
Establish Cooperation in the Classroom

Rudolf Dreikurs, M.D., Pearl Cassel, M.Ed.,
and Eva Dreikurs Ferguson, Ph.D.

John Wiley & Sons Canada, Ltd

National Library of Canada Cataloguing in Publication

Dreikurs, Rudolf, 1897-1972.
    Discipline without tears : how to reduce conflict and establish cooperation in the classroom/ Rudolf Dreikurs, Pearl Cassel and Eva Dreikurs Ferguson.

Rev. ed.
Includes index.
ISBN 0-470-83508-7

    1. Classroom management. 2. School discipline. 3. Discipline of children.
I. Cassel, Pearl, 1931- II. Ferguson, Eva Dreikurs III. Title.

LB3013.D74 2004   371.102'4   C2004-902940-1

Production Credits:
Cover design: Ian Koo
Interior text design: Pat Loi
Printer: Tri-Graphic Printing Ltd.

Printed in Canada

10 9 8 7 6 5 4 3 2

Table of Contents

Acknowledgments

Dr. Rudolf Dreikurs was an inspiration and mentor to many teachers, psychologists and counselors, and he changed the lives of millions of parents and children. As an Adlerian mentor to one of us (Pearl Cassel), he provided core ideas that were written in the first edition of this book. As father and teacher to the other of us (Eva Dreikurs Ferguson), he inspired a life-long appreciation of and dedication to Adlerian psychology as a theory, a set of methods and a philosophy of life.

We wish to thank Tony Kirby and Ken Howey for their editing expertise in the preparation of this edition. Pearl Cassel also wishes to thank the many pupils in her classes who provided the teaching experiences that made this book possible.

The quotations at the start of each chapter are taken either from recorded speeches or are quotations from the writings of the late Dr. Rudolf Dreikurs.

Preface

Pearl Cassel was an experienced teacher of 15 years when she wrote the first edition of *Discipline without Tears*. While attending seminars by Dr. Rudolf Dreikurs, she discovered the Adlerian approach to teaching, which she then immediately implemented. An important part of this approach was the emphasis on a specially designed half-hour class discussion period, which was timetabled for once a week. This was of great benefit not only to the teacher, but also to the pupils and the community. Pearl invited parents to her home to study parenting skills for a five-week session, using the book *Children: The Challenge*, by Dreikurs and Soltz.

Shortly after putting this technique into action in her class of nine- and ten-year-olds, Cassel found the behavior of her pupils so much improved that her teaching time expanded. Since it became no longer necessary to spend half the lesson time reminding, reprimanding and disciplining students, she could introduce subjects rich in art and culture into the curriculum. Students had a variety of creative paths they could follow: composing music and songs, making movies and film strips, writing poetry, performing plays and learning ethnic dances. These pursuits and daily physical education were introduced into her school timetables.

With regular standardized testing, Cassel found that each student gained basic skill competencies in math, spelling, reading and English at double the normal speed. Average scores leaped from Grade 3 to Grade 6 in one year. The learning environment was quiet, harmonious, productive and happy. The students loved to come to school and Cassel's passion for teaching escalated.

This new edition is updated to respond to important legal (and other) changes in North American educational systems. Corporal punishment is now forbidden, and most physical contact between teacher and pupil is disallowed. Importantly, modern culture has helped teachers to realize they need more help in classroom management. By reading this book, teachers will find answers to many questions about how to cope in an ever-changing educational environment. In the period since the writing of the first edition of this book, men have taken on significant roles as teachers in elementary schools, which we view as a welcome development and which we acknowledge by referring to the teacher at times as "he" and at other times as "she". Multiculturalism, English as a second language and the integration of challenged students are creating constant new demands as well as opportunities for teachers, and the techniques described in this book are designed to alleviate difficulties in these and other teaching areas.

As the students start putting democratic principles to work (attention to task, improved listening skills, helping fellow students), they learn more enthusiastically, gain confidence and improve their own competency. As teachers implement the ideas and methods in this book, they are sure to find their teaching experience more rewarding.

Eva Dreikurs Ferguson has taught the theory described in this book to hundreds of university students and to professionals in many countries. Those who encounter Adlerian theory for the first time are initially skeptical that the methods work easily and well. They find to their amazement that human relationship difficulties, which they assumed to be intractable, can be resolved peacefully, painlessly and rather quickly. Once students and professionals learn the ideas in this book they usually indicate with deep appreciation that the principles and methods readily apply to all areas of their lives, in marriage, parenting and work relationships.

Like many teachers who were taught by Rudolf Dreikurs, Pearl Cassel expresses a deep gratitude to her mentor, who was the major exponent of Adlerian psychology following the death of Alfred Adler. Cassel feels privileged to have studied with and learned from Dr. Dreikurs.

Introduction

Teaching the Adlerian Way

Parisa has deliberately dropped her pencil for the fifth time this morning. Jamal refuses to finish his arithmetic and is scribbling on his paper. Julio has just thrown a spitball across the room, while Paula has withdrawn and continues to stare blankly out of the window.

Why?

All these children made choices, although not consciously, to behave in these ways in order to find their place in the class, to "feel belonging." The purpose of this book is to explain the reasons for the children's actions and logic and to help teachers recognize their own teaching styles, as well as to understand how to change their own—and their students'—behavior.

Many educators and teachers are confused. Some think that being permissive helps the child to express his needs and so stop the misbehavior. Not so: what a child is really learning in a permissive class is laissez-faire anarchy, not democracy. The children learn the philosophy of "I shall do my own thing" and "I will work only when there is something in it for me." Then we are bitterly disappointed when they openly declare their right to do anything they want with no respect or concern for the feelings of others.

On the other hand, in very strict autocratic classrooms, the children learn that power, prestige and profit are the only values that count. These autocratic ideas invariably lead to conflict. Moreover, on reaching adolescence, many young people will reject these values and rebel.

For the past ten thousand years we have lived in an autocratic society. Our children can be understood only if we first realize that the basic problem of our confused society is rooted in the rapid growth of democracy, for which we were neither trained nor prepared. This unfortunate ignorance is the crux and cause of most of the chaos in our schools.

Child rearing has always been based on tradition. Margaret Mead in her book on the South Sea Islanders, *From the South Seas*, describes a number of different societies, each of them raising children a different way and thus maintaining and promulgating different cultural patterns. In these tribes, children were raised in the same manner for hundreds of years. Both children and adults knew where they stood with each other. What is the difference between the Islanders and North Americans? Tradition! Our traditions have changed to a large extent during the past 50 years.

All living creatures know what to do with their young—except the parents of today. We parents and teachers must first build a new tradition if we want to live in a world of peaceful co-existence. This is particularly necessary in classrooms where the teacher has not been taught democratic leadership. Student fights with student; teacher fights with student. All have the mistaken belief that they can only find their place by being superior.

The established traditions of raising and teaching children, which stemmed from an autocratic society, are no longer effective in a democratic setting. We have to learn new forms of dealing with each other because our relationships have changed. The adult–child relationships in the past were characterized by dominance and submission. Today, equality is the only basis on which we'll ever be able to solve discipline problems effectively.

In this rapidly changing world we are witnessing a rebellion of all those who previously were dominated in an autocratic society—minorities, unions, women—who are now no longer blindly accepting the dictates of authorities. This is an inevitable evolution for participation in decision-making.

Hostilities in school and home will cease only when we share the decision-making process as equals. When this happens, parents and teachers will have a common goal, and our homes and schools will have responsible and respectful children.

What is equality? It is not being equal in size, age, position or intelligence. It is treating each other with equal respect. It is having the same respect for a child in grade 2 as you have for your mother. This is the kind of equality that brings your class peaceful co-existence and makes the whole world a better place to live in. The desire for equality and participation was fought for a long time in the political and legal arenas, but only very recently has it become more generally recognized as a necessary process in human relations at home, at work and in the classroom.

Centuries ago the nobles in England set up the Magna Carta in order to limit the power of the king. With the early settlers in North America and with the industrial revolution in Europe and elsewhere, increasing pressures were exerted by citizens who demanded to be treated equally by legislatures and courts. Workers didn't want to be dictated to by management. Racial minorities, women and various groups who had felt disenfranchised pressed tirelessly for legal changes in order to gain equality. Today, it is our children's turn to fight. Just as the other groups have won, or are in the process of winning, their battle for equality, so will the children. They are in the majority and have time on their side. They want to be treated as equals and with equality of respect.

The Five Principles of Alfred Adler

The fundamental premises that underlie the ideas and methods of this book were formulated by Alfred Adler, a Viennese psychiatrist. Adler worked with children in the public schools in Vienna and described his ideas in *The Education of Children* (1957). He wanted his ideas to be part of every person's way of living, and he wrote books that could be understood by anyone, like *The Science of*

Living, originally published in 1929, and *What Life Should Mean to You,* published in 1931. His concept of the "iron-clad logic of social living" implies the recognition of human equality. Without this recognition we will not be able to solve our conflicts and develop harmonious living. He explained the personality structure that enables us to live as free democratic people and proposed a set of sound basic psychological premises that fit democratic principles. These can be most helpful to parents and teachers who want to know what democracy means.

His five basic premises on human conduct are:

1. People are social beings and their main desire is to belong. This is true for adults and children alike.

2. All behavior is purposive. One cannot understand the behavior of another person unless one knows to which goal it is directed, and it is always directed towards finding one's place. If an adult or child misbehaves, then it indicates that he or she has wrong ideas about how to be significant.

3. People are decision-makers. We decide what we really want to do, often without being aware of it. We are not merely victims of forces converging on us, such as heredity, environment or other outside influences. It is the realization that we can determine what we want to do that is the basis for our corrective and therapeutic optimism. Life history is important but cannot be used as an excuse for poor behavior.

4. Each person is a whole being who cannot be understood by some partial characteristics. We explain actions on the basis of the whole person. The whole is different than the sum total of the parts. (This is a very important theoretical prerequisite because it permits us to perceive the whole individual without going into a lengthy exploration. We can perceive a "pattern" of behavior.)

5. We do not see reality as it is, but only as we perceive it, and this perception may be mistaken or biased.

A teacher must understand that if a child resists learning or misbehaves, the problem is not so much based in the child's personal maladjustment as it is that of a cultural predicament. Children are social beings who want to belong. Teachers must learn to use the group as an aid to recognize the mistaken goals of misbehavior in children. Most adults, when correcting children, only make matters worse because they do exactly what the child wants them to do—and they end up reinforcing the child's mistaken goals. Once teachers read this book and understand the significance of what we call the four mistaken goals, they can then reveal to misbehaving children what their goal is by asking them a certain sequence of questions. If this is done properly, the "recognition reflex" will follow. This indicates that the child suddenly realizes why she is misbehaving, and that alternatives are opened for her to change her behavior. The word "goal" in this sense refers to human relations rather than tasks.

The teacher is a group leader. She creates the atmosphere, integrates all the diverse personalities and stimulates the democratic process. The class discussion in the classroom has the same benefits that families can have by using family meetings, also called "the family council," in their homes.[1] Classroom meetings train children in participatory democracy.

The alliance of parents, teachers and children participating in a true democracy can bring peace and harmony to our homes and schools, and ultimately to our society. The teaching profession, above all others, can use and teach democratic principles in our schools, in order to eliminate destructive hostilities in our lives.

NOTE

1. Family meetings are described by B.L. Bettner & A. Lew, *Raising Kids Who Can* (Newton Centre, Mass: Connexions Press, 1996).

Chapter One

Why the Tears?

Equality means that people, despite all their individual differences and abilities, have equal claims to dignity and respect.

—R. Dreikurs & V. Soltz, *Children: The Challenge*

Today, school systems are in a dilemma regarding discipline. The controversy over administering punishment cannot and will not be resolved until we give teachers alternative effective techniques for dealing with children who misbehave and refuse to learn. Until this happens, misbehaving children prevent the teacher from teaching and fellow students from learning. *Misbehavior becomes a violation of social freedoms.*

It is relatively easy to teach a class in which children want to listen, learn and behave, but every class has at least a few youngsters who do not fit this category—and herein lies the problem. When an ongoing discipline problem arises, often the teacher feels helpless to resolve the issue. While the last resort of sending a pupil to the principal's office gives the insecure teacher a certain amount of courage and confidence to face each challenging day, this is only a stopgap measure. Currently, most schools emphasize that teachers themselves should manage discipline issues (and the principals have become the last resort). Thus, more than ever, teachers must have new skills as an effective substitute action. Guidance counselors at the junior and primary level could be most helpful to teachers in developing a preventative mental health program, but cutbacks in educational spending have limited these opportunities. Elementary school children also need individual or group counseling when they have problems. If we wait until their troubles are big enough to take them out of our schools, or into our law courts, it is too late to redirect their early mistaken goals.

With mainstreaming, normalizing and other modern educational philosophies, classrooms have an ever-increasing range of ability and learning programs. We find children are grouped for instruction, yet our teachers are not trained to use group dynamics and sociometric testing. The teacher must learn these skills before grouping the children for an enterprise, project or creative work.

Often pupils are confronted with social problems because of the need to collaborate and work together toward an outcome. The teacher may not have trained them to get along and learn together in a democratic setting. The traditional teaching methods in which the teacher was an autocratic boss who used force, pressure, competition and a threat of punishment are now outdated. Even the pupils themselves will not accept this kind of leadership any more. If they are not given the opportunity to get involved in a participatory classroom democracy, they either rebel in class, or at home, or against society in general.

Many teachers have decided to change their autocratic ways and try the democratic approach. However, because there has been no one to teach them the new skills of becoming democratic leaders, they have become permissive anarchists. Their classrooms have become chaotic. Their pupils do what they want, learn what and when they want, care only occasionally for the needs of others, and have little respect for the teacher, school or friends. Both teacher and pupils have become discouraged. But permissiveness is not restricted to teachers. Parents, in seeking to avoid an autocratic approach, have mistakenly adopted methods that indulge their children and allow sleep-deprived, self-centered behavior at home.

We know that when children are discouraged they tend to misbehave, have no respect for order and learn very little. These classrooms of laissez-faire anarchy are producing a generation of tyrants whose prime aim and value is to do their own thing with not enough social awareness or consideration of their responsibility to contribute to society. Permissive teachers have abdicated their responsibility to teach. They have made the mistake of thinking that children should be allowed to learn whatever they want. Actually, teachers should motivate children to learn what they need to learn—which in primary grades are the basic skills of reading, language and arithmetic, and the social skills of living and learning in a group.

In a well-organized primary classroom, where the teacher is skilled in stimulating the students to learn what they need to learn, there are few discipline problems. If the teacher believes in educating the whole child, there is ample opportunity for the development and expression of creativity through art, music, dance and the language arts. When a problem arises, the teacher immediately asks herself some questions. Was the assigned work too difficult for some, or was it too easy and consequently boring? Was the lesson preparation adequate? Was the presentation stimulating and exciting? Was it too long or too short? Have the pupils been given sufficient time to finish, and are there opportunities for fast workers to do challenging enrichment? The way in which the teacher answers these questions indicates what action she can take to improve the situation.

If she is satisfied that her teaching methods are suitable, she may next go to the "hidden curriculum" for some answers. In that hidden curriculum may live a child with a health problem, either physical (for instance, impaired sight or hearing) or mental (such as traumas from having a drug-addicted parent); a recent disappointment such as a death of a pet; or an exciting anticipation of a happy event like a birthday party. The teacher should be aware of the difference between a temporary upset or excitement and a deeper, more permanent, problem.

When a teacher really knows her class, she is sensitive to the pupils' reactions, and if a personal problem is the cause of a disturbance, she is able to offer effective guidance. However, if disturbing behavior or resistance to learning is repetitive, she can learn to diagnose the purpose of the child's mistaken goals, to understand the private logic of the child and to redirect his behavior.

We pinpoint four mistaken goals that lead children to misbehave, and so the diagnosis and treatment are fairly simple, and the methods of dealing with them will be fully explained (see Chapter 6, "The Teacher–Parent Conference"). By using these methods, an elementary teacher can prevent most of the personality problems that, later, trouble our high schools and our society.

Structure and the Democratic Leader

In many of our primary school classrooms, children are learning at different levels and rates of progress; consequently, classes have become less structured. Professional thoroughness is no longer possible when all pupils are being taught different things at the same time. Few teachers have the time or energy to provide enrichment on top of the lessons. To provide some assistance in these circumstances, the following chapters will introduce teachers to specific methods of class management.

In open work areas, children are exposed to a variety of situations each day. They may work in small groups for basic skills and larger groups for creative experience, or find themselves with a hundred others during a team teaching presentation or alone for individual instruction. As teaching situations demand continual adjustments and require that students move from place to place, various kinds of problems may crop up. Some children cannot cope. They find it difficult to learn in this system, and they react unfavorably. Often they disturb the climate for the others. The misbehavior of even one child can disturb the atmosphere of the whole class. The dilemma is that children are gaining freedom without learning an accompanying sense of responsibility.

All children need structure to feel secure, and often they do not receive this at home. Teachers should provide some time each day in which a specific lesson is given to all members of the class, for instance music or history. This produces cohesiveness in the classroom. Even the challenged student will get a much needed sense of belonging from attending to a teacher's regular presentation. This helps the disadvantaged students with learning disabilities, who often feel left out because they have to work alone on their own prescribed learning programs.

Without structure, many of the old traditional values of teaching get lost. Students may become lazy, noisy, inconsiderate, and irresponsible. Work habits become sloppy; workbooks are badly written and inaccurate. With the lessening of structure, we can expect a lowering of academic standards instead of the anticipated improvement. Later, such students enter high school without sufficient reading skills to handle their courses. No wonder teachers are confused and discouraged.

Teachers have not been trained to teach the skills of living in a democracy. In this context, they have little knowledge of problem-solving and decision-making techniques, as shown by the research of Kurt Lewin.[1] Anarchy follows when autocratic control is lifted. In our contemporary society children live in such anarchy. They reject the disciplines, ethics, ideas and values of adults; they often live in a bewildered state, either of excessive materialism or an unbridled idealism that lacks social interest or a satisfying sense of contribution. But there is no ill of democracy that cannot be cured by more democracy, and to begin this cure, our teachers must learn to become democratic leaders.

In some jurisdictions in North America, standardized testing is in place for measuring levels of achievement in reading, math and English. It's important that teachers, parents and students know the level at which the student has competency; only then can appropriate programming be provided.

In the Province of Ontario, for example, standardized testing was reinstated in 1998. Since that time student scores have improved each year. For instance, the number of Grade 3 students meeting the provincial standard in math has increased by 35 percent between 1997–98 and 2001–01. This is a huge achievement.

The Overtired Child: A New Social Problem

Many students come to school tired. Sleep deprivation prevents them from learning and behaving appropriately. Their weakened immune systems lead to low-grade ear and throat infections. The tired child can fall victim to allergies, germs and viruses.

In today's society, where either single mothers or both parents go to work, there is considerable guilt on parents' part about not being there for the kids during the day. This can lead to overcompensation—indulging children for excessive periods of time during the free evening hours. Single mothers need to attend to their own life, and partners themselves need to spend quality time together. It's no wonder that many single parents get exhausted or that marriages collapse due to this unhealthy child-centered attitude.

It is quite common for parents to "entertain" their kids until 11 p.m. This is at least three hours past a healthy bedtime for most seven-to-eleven-year-olds. The children would be better equipped to learn at school if their home time with parents was restricted to one hour of quality time.

Many families have become so child-dominated that normal household courtesies and interaction with other family members go by the board. Instead of telephone calls to friends and family, the sterile email becomes the only means of communication. The warm sharing of an extended family is not a consistent part of many adults' or children's lives.

How can elementary teachers help in this situation? They need to send very strong, but diplomatic, messages to parents. They can also enlist the help of the children, perhaps by checking each morning to find out when each child went to bed the previous evening, and encouraging an earlier bedtime.

By handling a sleep deprivation problem effectively, everyone benefits—the child, the parent(s) and the teacher.

NOTE

1. K. Lewin, *Resolving Social Conflicts* (New York: Harper & Row, 1948).

Chapter Two

What Kind of Teacher Are You?

Nothing is as pathetic as a defeated authority who does not admit to that defeat.

—R. Dreikurs

Do you, as a teacher, believe that imposing your will on children is the only way you can control a class? A teacher who is committed to "making" pupils do as they are told, forcing them to learn, berating them when they don't, punishing any misdemeanor and denying any creative freedom of expression is one who is autocratic and tyrannical.

If you think that you know all the answers and have the attitude that you have the power to command children to do your will, you will sooner or later be defeated. Granted, the exercise of power, pressure and punishment to demand cooperation was traditionally viewed as the correct approach in the profession. Today, a teacher who imposes his or her ideas with a sharp voice and assumes the sole responsibility of making all decisions and setting all the rules for the class is a relic from a past that is not viable today.

Children today do not accept this kind of tyranny. They are aware of the present democratic atmosphere and expect to be treated as responsible, worthwhile, decision-making human beings. They resent being treated with scorn, and react with hostility and vengeance to outwit a domineering boss. From this lack of mutual respect they are quick to learn, firstly, a double standard, and secondly, that power of any kind is of prime importance.

Some children retaliate with mockery, stubbornness, temper-tantrums, disobedience, argument and a refusal to learn. As a child develops these behavior patterns, he becomes a troublemaker, dropout and potential delinquent. Most of our problem teenagers today are living in an arrested state of selfishness with no developed sense of responsibility toward a task or toward other persons. To a peer group they may be loyal, but they have no respect for anyone younger or older, or who holds different opinions. Many of these youngsters could have been saved by democratic teachers and counselors, but instead they have been discouraged by autocratic, insensitive people.

You have probably decided that you are not the tyrannical teacher who creates an atmosphere in which only a few "good" children become better, many "bad" children become worse and the majority of children are regulated by fear. In this type of environment the "good" children often strive to excel, but only to feel superior in order to look down on their classmates. They are not learning for the joy of it nor developing a willingness to meet the needs of any situation with a sense of contributing to the good of all.

Maybe you are not the autocratic tyrant who makes the "bad" child worse by punishing or discouraging him. Perhaps you do not have a class where there is little willing cooperation, where creativity is stifled, and social and emotional growth is arrested. But are you too permissive? Were you at one time autocratic and now have swung from one extreme to the other? Perhaps you have given up control completely and now live with stress and exasperation as the children control you.

As a permissive teacher, you do not regard any child as wrong; you condone everything each child does with the idea that each will turn out eventually to be a good and worthwhile member of society. You believe in providing numerous learning experiences in the classroom that pupils may choose to use. You suggest that they select their own topics or lessons for the day. You provide students with varieties of visual aids that they may use at will. You permit them to work in groups or individually or at the computer.

Some pupils may choose not to take a reading lesson for weeks, but you are confident they will ask you to teach them to read when they are ready. You don't really plan work for the pupils because you believe they can learn so much more from doing research projects about things that interest them. You don't bother to give tests because the students are all learning at different levels.

You may wonder at the end of the day what you have taught and why your head aches so much, but you pretend that a noisy classroom indicates that children are communicating and learning from one other. You get anxious when you are asked to write a report card, or meet a parent for an interview, because you really don't have any marks or grades to help give an accurate evaluation. In fact, you wonder if Megan has really made any continuous progress at all, or has permanently stagnated. Perhaps you are worried that she has even regressed. You may even be depressed and sick.

At the end of the term, there seem to be many materials lost or broken and many children fighting. They disrespect the rights of others, are tired, bored, one-track-minded and unable to cope with any routine at all. In effect, your class has become a totally self-centered group.

Parents are asking what is going on in your class because their youngsters seem to know less than they did last year and their behavior at home is so uncontrollable. Several of your children are now regularly visiting counselors, psychologists or even private psychiatrists. In general these young children are confused and don't know which end is up. They really believe they have a right to do exactly as they please and tyrannize their classmates, parents and even you. That is what you have led them to believe.

You think back, "I decided not to be an authoritarian. I read what the educational experts advised; I am a progressive teacher. But, deep in my heart, I know I really did abdicate my responsibility to teach that class, and I know most of those children could have learned to read, write and do math much better. I did not help them to solve life's problems. They cannot do meaningful project research because they cannot read the research books and I have not taught them the necessary skills. The children used to be my friends; now they disrespect me, the school, the community and even themselves. They are misbehaving because they are discouraged, and I'm discouraged, too. I am very confused because I don't know what I did wrong. Shall I leave the teaching profession? Does the work I am doing inevitably lead me to be unhappy and frustrated? Am I any good at what I do?"

Of course, this whole story is a nightmare. That permissive teacher is not really you. That teacher was *laissez-faire* and as a result had anarchy in the classroom. Your class does not fit that pattern.

If you are not an autocrat and not an anarchist, what can you be?

The alternative for you is to be a good democratic leader; that is, a leader who is kind but firm, who motivates pupils to learn what they ought to learn, who encourages pupils when they make mistakes, who maintains order and routine by letting each child participate in decision making.

The following are two approaches, with comparisons that distinguish the autocratic teacher from the democratic:

Autocratic	**Democratic**
Boss	Leader
Sharp voice	Friendly voice
Commands	Invites
Exerts power	Exerts influence
Pressures	Stimulates
Demands cooperation	Wins cooperation
I tell you what you should do	I tell you what I will do
Imposes ideas	Sells ideas
Dominates	Guides
Criticizes	Encourages
Finds fault	Acknowledges achievement
Punishes	Helps
Dictates	Discusses
I decide; you obey	I suggest, and help you decide
Sole responsibility of boss	Shared responsibility in team achievement

The characteristic difference between the two approaches is that the autocratic left column indicates pressure from without, the democratic right column represents stimulation from within. This fundamental difference permits you to evaluate your own "democratic index" and to examine every step you take and every approach you use.

The teacher who is a democratic leader uses group dynamics, teaches responsibility by giving responsibility, and provides a mentally healthy learning atmosphere for academic, emotional and social growth for every class member, which includes the teacher himself. That democratic teacher could—and should—be you.

Teacher Self-Evaluation

Teachers have many obligations and sometimes find themselves with conflicting pressures and values. On the one hand they need to enhance their pupils' learning and skills in ways that the larger society requires. On the other hand, they are expected to nurture the well-being of the children and to help their pupils become socially and emotionally mature. Conscientious teachers often find that the demands on their skills and energy exceed their capabilities and strengths. To help teachers develop their inner resources that are equal to the challenges teachers face, the following steps for self-evaluation are offered. Using these steps, teachers are likely to discover areas of strength they previously had not recognized and to highlight areas that need to be improved. Self-understanding enables teachers to be more effective and self-confident in the classroom.

The following are 12 recommended self-evaluation steps:

1. **Emotional stability—sound mental health**

    A sense of personal worth, self-respect and emotional security are essential. Ask yourself:

    · Do I value my own personal worth?
    · Do I recognize each child's individual personal worth?

- Do I treat all students with respect, politeness, understanding and patience?
- Do I teach reliability and cooperation?
- Do I have a sense of humor?

2. **Physical health—dynamic personality**

   Good teachers are fit, work at preventing illness and take good care of their bodies in order to teach at optimum levels. Your pupils need you well and enthusiastic in the classroom. Ask yourself:

   - Do I have high energy?
   - Do I eat sensibly?
   - Do I exercise regularly?
   - Is my appearance clean and attractive?
   - Am I enthusiastic in the classroom?
   - Do I motivate my pupils to want to learn?

3. **Good use of my intelligence and good teaching ability**

   Good teachers make effective use of their intelligence and are sensitive to the needs of others; grasp and understand subject knowledge; are patient with slower minds and recognize and can re-explain different solutions. Ask yourself:

   - Do I know what to expect from different pupils?
   - Am I careful to avoid registering my annoyance or frustration by word or gesture?
   - Do I develop remedial programs for slow learners?
   - Can I deal effectively with behavior problems?

4. **Creativity, imagination, resourcefulness**

   Good teachers are well informed and constantly research new educational material; seek and sift new ideas and apply effective ones and assess teaching effectiveness by testing pupils regularly, reviewing and re-teaching if necessary. Ask yourself:

- Do I set goals and objectives in lessons?
- Do I have a vision of what individual pupils can accomplish?
- Can I invent new ways of illustrating concepts?
- Have I tried more than one approach when a pupil is confused?
- Am I constantly obtaining fresh material from both likely and unlikely sources?
- Do I display ingenuity in obtaining pertinent materials?
- Can I set up room displays, establish classroom rules and regularly conduct class discussions?

5. **Courtesy, kindness, sympathy and tact**

   Courtesy promotes understanding and empathy; kindness sweetens communication and tact indicates knowledge of problem solving. Ask yourself:

   - Is my courtesy, or lack of courtesy, reflected in pupils' behavior?
   - Do pupils have rapport with me and trust me?
   - Do pupils react and respond with enthusiasm to my teaching?

6. **Sincerity and honesty**

   Trust is built on sincerity and honesty; a desire to help must be evident, and promises must be kept. Ask yourself:

   - Is my rapport one of honesty and are my expectations realistic?
   - Do pupils understand what I want from them?
   - Do pupils want to cooperate with one another and with me?

7. **Firmness**

   Firmness should not harden into rigidity, but your presentations should be carefully structured and delivered in a clear manner in order to create a secure learning environment. This calls for setting definite standards for good classroom life and solving any problems that arise at the weekly class discussion. Ask yourself:

   - Do my pupils respect me and also feel warmth for me?
   - Are my pupils always aware of what I expect of them?
   - Do my pupils know which decisions are final and best for their safety?

8. **Promptness, efficiency and organization**

   Effective teachers do planning and organization well in advance and make orderly plans for both formal and informal discussions. Ask yourself:

   - Do all my lessons start and end within allotted times?
   - Is my lesson and day plan organized ahead of time?
   - Do pupils sense my organization and respond accordingly?

9. **Positive, encouraging attitude**

   Being positive will bring out the best in your pupils, thus producing happier classes. It also indicates your ability to concentrate on pupils' learning styles. Ask yourself:

   - Do I acknowledge good progress?
   - Are pupils gently encouraged to do better when they make mistakes?

10. **Democratic leadership**

    Although a teacher is the responsible authority in the classroom, he or she uses guidance and directives from principals, specialists and superintendents. Ask yourself:

- Do I communicate well with my pupils?
- Are my pupils entrusted to carry out simple classroom maintenance tasks?
- Taking into consideration my pupils' ages and stages of development, do my pupils share in the decision-making process by proposing ideas, carrying out suggestions or organizing activities?

11. **Professional status**

    Responsible teachers establish friendly relations with colleagues, and further their academic training and professional development. Ask yourself:

    - Do I read educational magazines and other related material?
    - Do I attend conferences, conventions or seminars?

12. **The basic qualities of a good teacher**

    A good teacher is patient, loving and kind; gives directions clearly and expects pupils to listen quietly and attentively; in line with the "4R" concept of Raymond Corsini,[1] a good teacher is Responsible, Resourceful, Reasonable and Responsive; and can instill these four R's in students' attitudes and behavior. Ask yourself:

    - Am I behaving in a responsible manner?
    - Am I resourceful in finding enrichment materials for gifted pupils?
    - Do I make reasonable requests?
    - Am I responsive verbally, or with actions, to pupils' needs?

If you can answer most of these questions in the affirmative you and your pupils are likely to experience school as a positive place for learning, and happily look forward to going to school each day.

NOTE

1.Pearl Cassel and Raymond Corsini, *Coping with Teenagers in a Democracy* (Toronto: Lugus, 1990).

Chapter Three

A Rewarding Alternative: Teaching the Democratic Way

That is the meaning of democracy: respect and dignity for every citizen....The obvious trend of evolution leads to a conception of living together without force and suppression.

—R. Dreikurs, *The Challenge of Marriage*

One can think of discipline as the fulcrum of education. Without discipline, both teacher and pupil become out of balance and very little learning takes place. Today's discipline problems can be overcome if we turn from the obsolete autocratic method of demanding submission from students and accept a new order based on the principles of freedom and responsibility. Teachers should be neither permissive nor punitive. What you have to learn is how to become a match for your students, wise to their ways and capable of guiding them without letting them run wild or alternately stifling them.

The successful formula for guiding children in the classroom is based on the belief that democracy is not just a political ideal, but a way of life. It is part of human relationships that contain dignity and mutual respect. This democracy has freedom but not license. It is a shared responsibility that must be taught. You enjoy the freedoms and accept the responsibilities of living in a democracy. Before you became a teacher, you learned many skills that provided you with a freedom of choice, and you chose to work with children. That freedom was not license. If you had cried, "I want to be free," and your teachers had complied and not taught you skills, you would now be shackled by your own chains of ignorance. It is what you learn that allows you to be free.

Here is an example. Imagine that you are at a holiday resort. The sports director suggests a variety of activities such as swimming, tennis, badminton, water-skiing, golf, sailing, dancing and bridge. Because you have been taught certain skills, you have the freedom to choose from all these activities, or you may prefer to relax and just enjoy the sun. Now think of the person who has not learned these skills. She has no freedom to choose; she really has no choice but to lie in the sun. She may be thinking, "I wish I could swim, play tennis or golf, etc.," but because she has never learned these skills, she is actually restricted.

A person who is truly free has learned a wide variety of academic, artistic, athletic and social skills. Most of these were taught at school. Through cooperation, a willingness to learn and an opportunity to exercise appropriate decision making, this individual truly develops an ability to use free choice in any situation. Without these skills you are extremely limited and forced into an environment devoid of choice. We have all seen the misery caused by an individual's inability to use problem-solving techniques to make appropriate decisions, an inability that badly affects friendships and family life.

Without learned skills, courage and a sense of responsibility, you have no true freedom of choice, to work or play, or to be rich or poor. Freedom requires skills and responsibility. To be truly free means to be independent (economically and emotionally) and to use the power of self-determination. You have experienced this kind of freedom, and from a variety of career possibilities, you have chosen to teach.

If you are a democratic teacher you will be extending your philosophy of freedom to your pupils, by assuming your role, not as an autocrat, nor as a permissive anarchist, but as a responsible guide. Your pupils will be learning skills with enthusiasm and developing social awareness by enjoying the feeling of contributing and being useful. You leave the classroom each evening confident that you have lived and learned with your pupils through an exciting, challenging day. You relax, enjoy yourself and look forward to another day of lively experience with your pupils. Your freedom helps your students learn how to become free.

How did you reach this idyllic state? You have learned that the mental health of any teacher depends on the following six realizations:

1. You guard your physical health with periodic checkups because you are aware that the constant effort of teaching and maintaining good interpersonal relationships requires your maximum energy. (The class of a sick teacher is sure to suffer in spite of her best efforts to be pleasant and well prepared.)

2. You like children and really enjoy teaching.

3. You understand and accept yourself with a sense of self-worth that protects you from being easily hurt or upset. You have the courage to be imperfect. You can accept criticism and even laugh at yourself sometimes.

4. You work for a sense of accomplishment and are stimulated to be imaginative.

5. You accept new challenges with confidence and courage, and always put forth a genuine effort.

6. You reserve time to take the opportunities for growth and development. Your lively interest in a number of activities, not necessarily connected with education, keeps you young and alert. Recreation in some form of play or hobby is an effective means of emotional release and self-expression. Tensions and frustrations are part of life and need to be relieved actively.

You are also aware of three signs of danger that may eventually cripple your mental health:

1. If you are overly anxious, you may be heading for severe difficulty in the classroom. The burdens of anxiety and guilt will lead to feelings of insecurity that the students will then also feel, and the result will diminish a sense of confidence and security of the class. This can become a vicious circle with the discomfort of each aggravating the other.

2. If you are feeling desperately bored or caught in a rut, you may be dying mentally. When the life of a teacher has lost its sparkle the whole morale of the class will sag.

3. If you find yourself hating the thought of going to school every morning or feeling resentful toward your students or fellow staff members, you're headed for emotional and bodily reactions of stress. If you are feeling miserable, trying to maintain a happy expression and a tolerant attitude is a tension-producing strain. Children watch for facial clues and are quicker than adults to detect insincerity. You can't fool them for long.

If you apply the following ten points, you'll promote acceptable behavior in a happy learning environment:

1. You are warm, friendly and kind, but firm.

2. You act and speak with confidence and sincerity, and express a sense of humor naturally.

3. You always have work well planned before the class starts.

4. You treat all the pupils with equal respect by listening to their opinions and considering their feelings.

5. You are encouraging at all times, in order to develop or restore the self-confidence of your pupils. By distinguishing between the deed and the doer, you never damage your

relationship with the children. You may object to what a child is doing, but not to the child himself. Never deny him the right to be respected as a person.

6. You are as impartial as possible. You try not to favor the pleasant, likeable child or reject the one who is provocative or deficient.

7. You are able to integrate the class as a whole or divide it for group instruction in order to promote optimum learning.

8. You encourage group discussion and participation in decision making, set boundaries for expected behavior and maintain these boundaries with effective stimulating teaching.

9. You are not mistake-centered, but always accent the positive, by marking only the correct answers. You give recognition for any genuine effort.

10. You rotate the class monitors weekly and involve all pupils in the chores and responsibilities of the classroom.

As a good democratic teacher you talk only when it is necessary and never fall into the educator's trap of talking too much. You know that nagging, preaching, repeating directions and criticizing is an absolute waste of "air time." Where discipline is concerned you know that quiet action is always more effective than words. All of your pupils talk freely in controlled discussion to develop their oral language skills, share ideas and opinions, express their creativity and plan certain class projects.

Your approaches are democratic and differ greatly from those used by the traditional autocratic teachers. You identify yourself as a group leader, not as a powerful boss. Your voice is friendly, not sharp. You win cooperation by influencing the class, rather than by demanding and using pressure. By stimulating a desire to learn, you sell ideas instead of imposing your will.

You think of guiding and helping the child, not dominating and punishing him. Every child in the class is invited to share the responsibilities of the group; you don't take on sole responsibility and demand the children's obedience. By offering suggestions, you help them make their own decisions. In all of these ways you stimulate from within, rather than exert pressure from without.

You occupy a crucial position in each child's life. Your influence is long lasting. After his parents, you are the first person to motivate the child's interest toward educational pursuits. You are responsible for setting an atmosphere in which each child's attitudes and achievements will grow with continuous progress.

Chapter Four

How Does a Child Grow?

The education of our children today is largely mistake-centered. They are exposed to a sequence of discouraging experiences, both at home and at school. Everyone points out what they did wrong as well as what they could do wrong. We deprive our children of the only experience that can really promote their growth and development—the experience of utilizing their own strengths.

— **R. Dreikurs**

Every child grows emotionally and socially as well as physically. Charts and other professional material have been published for teachers to describe different stages of a child's growth. The progression of the physical development is obvious; but we, as teachers, may be seriously trapped by concerning ourselves with a sequential approach to emotional and social growth, as described by Gesell and Piaget.[1]

Publications describing development can provide us with only an anticipation of certain behaviors and reactions, and this very anticipation may even lead a teacher to promote such reactions that possibly the child was not intending. We teachers may be putting negative words into his mouth or thoughts into his head. Children often behave in ways they believe adults expect. Think of the child as being stupid and she will behave stupidly. Think of her as being mature and she will rise to meet your expectations.

Kahlil Gibran understood children perfectly when he wrote:

Your children are not your children.
They are the sons and daughters of Life's longing for itself.
You may give them your love but not your thoughts,
For they have their own thoughts.
You may house their bodies but not their souls,
For their souls dwell in the house of tomorrow,
Which you cannot visit, not even in your dreams,
You may strive to be like them,
But seek not to make them like you.

We offer a simple yet comprehensive way of thinking about child development according to the four phases of development:

1. Life in the family before entering school

2. The elementary and middle school years

3. Adolescence

4. The final entry into adult society

From early infancy on and by means of trial and error, the young child actively seeks to make sense of his world. He not only is influenced by the significant persons in his life but he actively influences them. This mutual influence occurs from early infancy on. The child is not a passive recipient of others' actions but is instrumental in shaping their behavior. It is a transaction. Pampering and spoiling by parents may occur already in the first few months of life, and the child by his behavior can exaggerate this style of parenting.

In the family phase, the child develops his own concept about himself in his relationships and transactions with parents and siblings. This forms what Adler calls the child's "lifestyle."[2] In school the child socializes in a community with children from different families, many of whom speak a different language and possess different family values. As the child grows into adolescence, his peer group becomes his value-forming agent. At this teenage stage some youths may find difficulties in cognitive skills but thrive with new enjoyments in music, art, drama or physical education. In some cases, when high schools provide adequate time for these subjects, students become productively engaged and discipline problems diminish. By creating a code of conduct, schools working together with students and parents are likely to function more democratically and to have less truancy problems.

Every human, adult or child, is a social being. We all want to belong, to find our place in the group. Every action of the child is an endeavor to find her place. Some actions we accept as appropriate behavior. If these are given recognition the child will not become discouraged and switch to useless or destructive behavior. The child is an excellent observer but a poor interpreter. She watches all that goes on around her. She draws her own conclusions from what she sees and searches for guiding lines for her behavior. The growing child learns to make adjustments to her inner and outer environment. The mental health of any individual depends on the adjustments that she makes and her ability to cope with problems. A child living in an encouraging environment at school can make appropriate adjustments easily. Conversely, a child who experiences a discouraging environment is more likely to display poor adjustments, and experience poor mental health.

In Alfred Adler's early writings he discussed "organ inferiority," which is an expression of the way in which a child responds actively to his hereditary endowment. When a child is born with a certain weakness, he either develops a lasting deficiency in this area or, in order to make up for it, he develops an overcompensation of some form and may even develop special skills in the very area where his deficiency lies. For example: Jamica is born with a speech impediment and later becomes an accomplished public speaker. What determined this outcome? Her creativity, resolution and discipline. So, it is not the handicap that holds us back, but our attitude toward that handicap. So also, a healthy child with a behavior problem may either overcompensate or do the reverse, give up.

In many schools, intelligence and aptitude tests are given and the students' test scores are recorded and provided to teachers. This has led many teachers to have been influenced too strongly by these scores, which in some cases may not even be accurate measures. The consequences can be injurious, if teachers on the basis of such scores expect too much or too little achievement from their students. Our anticipation of a child's behavior, reaction or performance often produces the actual results we expect.

Because our expectations influence children profoundly, it is to everyone's advantage for us to expect all children to be responsible, contributing human beings with an intrinsic worth, deserving of respect. We as teachers are then more likely to find and develop that potential which is present in every growing child. As teachers of elementary school children, we should be particularly aware of this growing potential. Up to about the age of ten, problems in school can be resolved relatively easily when teachers know how to deal with them in ways described in this present book. School can serve to strengthen the child's skills, knowledge and self-esteem at any age, but the most far-reaching effects are in the elementary school years.

No child should ever be considered "hopeless," according to Adler. Any child who is told that she is a failure is being deprived of her dignity and as a result will lose respect for herself.

When we are fully aware of the influence we have on each of our pupils we should think of the example that we are showing them by our own attitudes and behavior (see Chapter 7, "Competition in an Elementary School"). We should also consider the following thoughts about how a child grows according to what he lives with:

If a child lives with criticism, he learns to condemn.

If a child lives with hostility, he learns to fight.

If a child lives with ridicule, he learns to be shy.

If a child lives with fear, he learns to be apprehensive.

If a child lives with shame, he learns to feel guilty.

If a child lives with tolerance, he learns to be patient.
If a child lives with encouragement, he learns to be confident.
If a child lives with acceptance, he learns to love.
If a child lives with approval, he learns to like himself.
If a child lives with recognition, he learns it is good to seek accomplishments.
If a child lives with honesty, he learns what truth is.
If a child lives with fairness, he learns justice.
If a child lives with security, he learns to have faith in himself and those around him.
If a child lives with friendliness, he learns the world is a nice place in which to live, to love and be loved.

NOTES

1. A. Gesell, *Child Development: An Introduction to the Study of Human Growth* (New Haven: Yale University Press, 1949).
J. Piaget, "Will and action." *Bulletin of the Menninger Clinic* 26 (3, 1962): 138–145.

2. A. Adler, *The Science of Living* (New York: Doubleday, 1969).

Chapter Five

Identifying and Correcting Misbehavior and the Four Mistaken Goals

*If training were as simple as setting a good example, we would not find so many irresponsible children coming from homes and schools where the parents and teachers are so responsible. So often, what we do to correct a child is responsible for his **not** improving.*

—R. Dreikurs

Usually, psychologists and psychiatrists concentrate on children who have problems and exhibit deviant behavior rather than working with "normal" children. Sometimes we wonder, "What is really normal?" As teachers, you know there are many variations of normal behavior, but you also have observed that a well-adjusted child will display most of the following characteristics:

- has a true sense of his own worth
- has a feeling of belonging
- has socially acceptable goals
- is able to meet the needs of a situation
- thinks in terms of "we" rather than just "I" (a self-centered child is discouraged and needs active guidance)
- assumes responsibility
- is interested in others
- respects the rights of others

- is tolerant of others
- cooperates with others
- encourages others
- is courageous
- is willing to share, rather than being concerned with "How much can I get?"
- is honest
- puts forth a genuine effort

You may be dismayed when you look at your pupils within the context of these ideal qualities, but don't be discouraged; children can be trained to cultivate their innate capacity for social interest, and to develop these "contributing" ways.

The Motives of Misbehavior

For a child to develop normally she should be encouraged by her parents, teachers, adult relatives, Cub Scout and Brownie leaders, church workers, neighbors and all adults with whom the child interacts. All adults who come into contact with a child can be either encouraging or discouraging. An adult who discourages a child is not helping the child, and with vulnerable children, this is very likely to lead to problems and to misbehavior.

Rudolf Dreikurs wrote with Don C. Dinkmeyer,

Encouragement is necessary for the child's development. He becomes what he is encouraged to become. Teachers must be made aware of the importance of assisting the child to his optimal development within his social setting.

Encouragement stimulates the child to do his best and enables him to recognize his abilities. The process of encouragement then extends beyond mere faith and belief in the individual to include the capacity for translating this faith and belief to the child. The child may not be perfect in his performance. But commending him on his effort enables him to grow through belief in himself and his abilities.

We should realize that a misbehaving child is only a discouraged child trying to find his place; he is acting on the faulty logic that his misbehavior will give him the social acceptance that he desires. We should avoid criticizing a misbehaving child, because our criticism just provokes hostility. A hostile child does not learn new behavior adjustments because he uses his emotions to block his learning processes. By maintaining a friendly relationship, we can discover the child's underlying reason for the mistaken behavior, the wrong concepts or assumptions, and then correct them.[1]

We should understand and always bear in mind that a misbehaving child is only a discouraged child trying to find her place; she is acting on the faulty logic that her misbehavior will give her the social acceptance that she desires.

We should avoid criticizing a misbehaving child, because our criticism will only provoke hostility. A hostile child does not learn new behavior adjustments because she uses her emotions to block her learning processes. By maintaining a friendly relationship, we can discover the child's underlying purpose for the mistaken behavior, the wrong concepts or assumptions, and then correct them.

Once we understand the goals of the child's behavior, we can practice effective methods of correction. Modifying just the behavior is not enough; we must modify her motivation. This may be done more easily with young children and is particularly effective with preschool children. However, teachers can help all children up to the age of ten to change their goals. (These methods are not always sufficient for the correction of older children. Teenagers require different methods. See *Coping with Teenagers in a Democracy,* by Pearl Cassel and Raymond Corsini in Appendix B, "Suggested Further Reading.")

In our culture, young children have few opportunities to make useful contributions toward the welfare of the family. Adults or perhaps older siblings do whatever needs to be done and the young child finds few ways to be useful and to help. It was easier for a child growing up on a farm, where there were many necessary chores to be performed, to feel that her part of the family work was a vital contribution. Nowadays, with our more affluent and urban way of life, many children make no real contribution to the welfare of others, and those who have regular chores to perform often become easily discouraged when they compare their inept performance with the more efficient rapid accomplishments of adults or older siblings. When both parents go to work and pick up fast food for supper, the children have little opportunity to help even with food preparation as a way of feeling significant.

The Four Mistaken Goals and How They Lead to Misbehavior

After observing thousands of children, many of whom showed a wide range of misbehavior, Rudolf Dreikurs identified the following as the four goals of children's misbehavior: (1) to get attention; (2) to get power; (3) to get revenge and (4) to purposefully display inadequacy.[2]

Many attempts to discover more than these four goals have, to date, proved unsuccessful. They are identified as mistaken goals, because the children make mistaken assumptions. It is important to know that some children show behavior that adults think is positive, like a child's taking the role of teacher's "special helper." It is important for adults to understand that such a child may have a mistaken goal, and one needs to understand the motivation and not look only at the behavior.

The child who "helps" only for the goal of attention may stop helping as soon as attention is not given. In contrast, the child who "helps" but whose goal is to contribute will continue to help even when her behavior does not bring attention. The goal of contribution is the appropriate goal, and children's mistaken goals need to be replaced by the goal of contribution.

The four mistaken goals refer to the purpose of a child's misbehavior. The goals are mistaken because the discouraged child wrongly believes that attaining the goal will lead to a feeling of belonging, for example, when children strive for the goal of attention, they believe that once they receive attention they have value and "belong." These goals are further mistaken because they are based on the child's faulty belief that she does not belong and does not have intrinsic value.

All children have intrinsic value. Their behavior may be of no positive value, but each child has positive value.

Changing the mistaken goals into the goal of "striving to contribute" enables children to give up their mistaken goals and to behave in mutually respectful, cooperative and constructive ways based on prosocial intrinsic motivation. One can label a goal and a behavior—but not the child herself.

What follows are techniques of modifying the motivation (the goal) rather than the behavior itself. When the motivation is changed, behavior of a more constructive nature follows automatically. In order to use this "Four-Goal Technique," the following steps must be taken.

1. Observe the child's behavior in detail.

2. Be psychologically sensitive to your own reaction.

3. Confront the child with the four goals in sequential order and listen as well as watch for the response.

4. Note the recognition reflex.

5. Apply appropriate corrective procedures.

Goal One—To Get Attention

When the child is deprived of the opportunity to gain status through his useful contributions, he usually seeks proof of his status in the class through getting attention. He employs this faulty logic: "Only if people pay attention to me do I feel belonging and have a place in this world."

Although the child does not know it, getting attention is not a way of developing self-confidence nor does it develop self-reliance. So, instead, the child develops an insatiable appetite for attention and requires ever-increasing amounts of it in a misguided attempt to "belong" and to be sure of his place. Usually the child first tries to find his place through pleasant and socially acceptable means. He may make "cute remarks" or do stunts. Often he gives the impression of excellence and this is a source of delight to many parents and teachers. Why, then, is it called "mistaken"? Because the child's goal is not to learn or to cooperate, but rather to elevate himself to gain special attention. This maladjustment becomes apparent when praise and recognition are not forthcoming. Then the "good"performance stops.

Attention-getting behavior can be constructive or destructive, passive or active. An active-constructive goal is seen in children who seek to be "first" or perfect and who work hard to gain attention for their good work. Children with such a goal are often rewarded by praise, rewards and awards, and they typically are thought of as model students and not identified as displaying "misbehavior." However, when the goal is one of superiority, the child is not intrinsically motivated by tasks or by the goal of contribution. Rather, the goal is self-glorification. When the anticipated rewards or praise do not occur, such a child can become easily discouraged and (when very young) turn either towards a passive-constructive goal or, more frequently, to more destructive methods of gaining attention. Often such children are vulnerable to the belief "If I cannot be the best, I'll be the worst," and when they do not attain first place they act destructively.

The passive-constructive goal is evident when the child's methods for getting attention are of a passive nature. Often such a child becomes a "teacher's pet." These attributes are quite socially acceptable, especially in girls. The "southern belle" appeals to others in her "helplessness" and thereby gains special attention and service, with a minimum of contribution or real effort.

Attention-getting demands keep increasing. Sooner or later many children are no longer satisfied with the amount of attention that they receive by using socially acceptable (constructive) means, so they become discouraged and switch to behaving in a negative way.

The active form of destructive attention-getting is labeled as a "nuisance" on tables 5.1 and 5.2 at the end of this chapter. This includes the "show-off" who becomes somewhat obnoxious, the "clown" who tends to bother us, the "mischief-maker," the "brat" who makes a nuisance of himself, and the child who keeps us constantly busy by asking questions, not for the information he receives, but to keep us occupied with him.

If the "charmer" type becomes discouraged in his first methods of passively keeping us busy, he usually switches to the useless-behavior side and becomes destructive in a passive way. We type the child as "lazy" as long as his goal is to get extra attention and service. These children manage to put others in their service by being "inept." They require adults to "help" them, and since children usually manage adults much better than adults manage children, the adults usually fall for their provocations. So we remind, coax, pick up after them, reassure them whenever they show fear and act in a way that only further reaffirms their faulty evaluation of their lack of ability.

For the child who is seeking attention as his goal in life, being ignored is intolerable. Rather than be ignored the child will accept punishment and even pain and humiliation, in order to get the extra attention or service for which he yearns. A teacher who falls for this, allows himself to be kept busy; he nags, coaxes, reminds, constantly advises and gives the child extra service. Then he feels annoyed at the child. Even if the child is using socially acceptable means of attention-getting, the teacher may at times feel that he is being kept unduly busy. By behaving in what the teacher believes is the "natural" way, he only fortifies the misbehaving child's faulty logic and reinforces the child's mistaken goal.

What can the teacher do?

He needs to redirect the child's goal from seeking special status and self-elevation towards one of cooperation, sharing, and accomplishing tasks for the intrinsic motivation of task accomplishment and joy of learning. He should only give the child positive attention at other times, *not* when the child is seeking it with behavior aimed at self-elevation. The teacher should recognize that an attention-seeking child, even one who is using constructive methods, is a somewhat discouraged child. The correction of all misbehavior is to encourage (*not* praise) the child. The teacher's role is to help the child who is using destructive methods to use constructive methods, and then further encourage him to find his place by making useful contributions to the group. In other words, help the child develop his "social interest" instead of giving him personal attention.

The shy child can be stimulated to more active behavior by a similar procedure. Ignoring his bid for special attention through his passivity—regardless of how charming or provocative it may be—and deliberately encouraging and commenting on any active effort, will persuade the child to change his approach. This will bring out the child's best efforts without any need for attention, praise or recognition.

Goal Two—To Get Power

If parents and teachers do not employ correct methods to stop the demand for undue attention, the child becomes a power-seeker. The power-seeking child wants to be the boss; she operates on this faulty logic: "If you don't let me do what I want, you don't love me," or "I only count when you do what I want you to do." In many ways the goal of power is similar to that of destructive attention-getting, but it is more intense.

The active type, labeled "Rebel" in table 5.1 (at the end of this chapter), often argues, contradicts, lies, may have violent temper tantrums, refuses to do what she is told to do, continues forbidden acts and may refuse to do her work and is openly disobedient. If the child is of the passive type, her laziness is much more pronounced than in the attention-getting goal (goal 1), so that she usually does no work at all, or she "forgets," becomes stubborn and is passively disobedient.

The teacher's reaction to a power-seeking child is to feel that his own leadership is threatened. He thinks, "Who is running this class? This child or me?" The teacher vows, "She can't get away with this; I won't let her do this to me!" But the teacher's efforts to control or force a power-drunk child are usually futile. The child will win about 99 percent of the time, and if the teacher succeeds in overcoming and defeating her, the child usually becomes even more rebellious and may then seek revenge. If the teacher wins the struggle today, the child will usually win tomorrow. No final victory is possible. The longer the power struggle continues, the more the child becomes convinced that power has value, and thus her mistaken goal of finding her place is reinforced.

The child's "faulty logic" will not convince an adult, but it makes sense to the child. She still wants to belong, although her methods to seek her place do not have the effect of winning friends.

What can the teacher do to help the child correct her mistaken convictions? The teacher may as well admit to the child, and to the class, that the child is a powerful person. If the teacher fights with her, the child will win. Nobody is obliged to fight with a child. Many do, because they think they can win. But the teacher should avoid getting into a power struggle and should extricate himself from the conflict.

A safe way to deal with the situation would be to recognize that the power-seeking child is always ambitious and try to redirect her ambition towards useful channels. She might be enlisted to help another child, or be given a position of responsibility that she feels has some prestige. (Give guidance so the child won't abuse her position.) Rather than threatening the child, the teacher may appeal to her for help. The teacher may even say, "I know I cannot make you do it." This may disarm the child and enlist her cooperation.

An appeal to this type of child for advice and assistance will be more effective than threats. If the teacher acknowledges the child's power and ability to defeat him, the teacher "takes his sail out of the child's wind" and there is no longer any use in the child's "blowing."

The fact that a power-seeking child has the skill and energy, as many such children do, to be able to upset adults at home and at school in often ingenious ways is a clue to how effective such a child could be when redirected to a socially responsible goal. Such a child, when striving for a goal of contribution instead of a goal of power, can achieve enormous accomplishments of value to the group.

Goal Three—To Get Revenge

If a child feels so beaten down that he no longer seeks to win the power struggle, but seeks to retaliate, he will use Goal 3—revenge.

The revenge-seeking child is so deeply discouraged that he feels that only by hurting others, as he feels hurt by them, can he find his place. He views life itself and other people as grossly unfair. Convinced that he is hopelessly disliked, he wants to counter-hurt. He responds with deep distrust to the teacher's efforts to convince him otherwise. Since his goal is to hurt others as he feels hurt by them, the child is seemingly "unlovable." His actions are vicious, violent and brutal. He is openly defiant and is a potential delinquent, if not already one. The child knows the vulnerability of others, whom he sees as opponents, and he is out to hurt them. He considers it a victory when he is labeled vicious, as this seems to be the only triumph open to him. The revenge-seeking child may injure his classmates, animals and adults. He may scratch, bite and kick. He is a sore loser and immediately starts plotting revenge if he is defeated, usually by even more violent methods than those used before.

Leaders of youth street gangs usually resort to Goal 3. A goal of revenge can be seen in adolescents and adults as well as children. These revenge-seekers see the whole of society as their enemy and frequently look down on others with contempt. Yet underneath the facade they are deeply discouraged individuals who possess little hope for themselves. Usually they are active, but occasionally we find one who is sullen and defiant in a "violent passivity," and this type is even more deeply discouraged. Children who use Goal 3 are very difficult to deal with and may require professional help, in addition to anything the teacher may be able to do. Punishment will only produce more rebellion, so it is to be avoided. "Logical consequences" (see Chapter 7, "Competition in an Elementary School") should not be used when the child is in a power contest (Goal 2) or seeking revenge (Goal 3). The main aim of the teacher should be to try to win the child over and persuade him that he can be liked by others, including his peers and his teachers. This is difficult because much of his behavior will deny that this is possible. When the child seeks revenge, he is not making it easy for others to like him or to show him affection. However, rejecting the child makes the problem only worse, because it convinces him how unfair life is and how unlovable he is.

Methods are needed to counteract his beliefs. The class as a group may be enlisted to help, but the teacher must take steps to assure that the group will not make things worse by turning against the discouraged child. "Good" children often enlist themselves in an alliance with the teacher against the "bad" children; this situation must be avoided. Group discussions *can* promote mutual understanding and help the child. Sometimes the teacher may enlist the help of another child who may have some empathy for the discouraged child and may be willing to be a "buddy" to him. (For further suggestions, see Chapter 13, "Typical Problems in the Classroom and Their Solutions.")

When the teacher understands that the revenge-seeking child himself feels very hurt and for this reason tries to hurt others, it is important for the teacher to feel concern and understanding and not to feel hurt.

Goal Four—To Display Inadequacy

The child who displays inadequacy has given up trying. A child who has tried passive-destructive forms of attention-getting in order to achieve the feeling of belonging may eventually become so deeply discouraged that she gives up all hope of significance and expects only failure and defeat. She has a feeling of hopelessness about finding a place. In addition, she may assume this position in order to avoid any further situation that might be embarrassing or humiliating to her. With very little self-esteem, she feels she must covetously guard what little she has. Thus, she uses her inability as a protective shield to appear disabled, or to avoid any test situation in which she might lose. (She displays an inferiority complex.)

Her actions appear "stupid" and she rarely participates; by her extreme ineptitude she prevents anything being demanded or expected of her. Many children who test and behave as mentally retarded are quite capable, but they are so deeply discouraged that they score badly and are then treated as if they were hopeless. They may be placed in special programs for children with low intelligence even though they actually may be of normal or high intelligence. They play "stupid" successfully. Some of these may be brilliant children but use Goal 4 in a mistaken attempt to cope with a world that they view as extremely discouraging. Being a victim and a pessimist can become a lifestyle.

It is very difficult for the teacher not to fall for the child's provocation that "you can't do anything with me so leave me alone." The natural reaction is for the teacher to give up. The child's discouragement is contagious, but it is important that the teacher not yield to this provocation as he is inclined to do. Great amounts of encouragement are needed and the child must be encouraged especially when she makes mistakes. Every possible attempt should be made to make the discouraged child feel worthwhile. The teacher is able to help best by having a sincere conviction that there is hope for the child and conveying that he will not give up on her, even though the child has given up on herself.

Various Kinds of Misbehaviors

The teacher may be surprised to notice a child switch from one kind of misbehavior to another. If the child switches to more disturbing behavior, this is likely to signal that the discouragement is growing worse. The four goals are the sequential result of discouragement.

In Goal 1 the child is less discouraged than in Goal 2. Goal 2 reflects less discouragement than Goal 3, and Goal 3 reflects less discouragement than Goal 4. As the child's behavior improves it changes in terms of goals and feelings of encouragement. The patterns vary, perhaps changing from Goal 3 to Goal 2 to Goal 1, and finally to normal contributing behavior. Goal 4 may only slowly change to Goal 1. The more discouraged the child is, the longer it will take to help the child to strive for a goal of cooperation and contribution. This may take as long as a year.

The most frequent deteriorating sequence of changes that result from deepening discouragement on the child's part are:

1. Active-constructive attention-getting, to

2. Active-destructive attention-getting, to

3. Active-destructive power, to

4. Active-destructive revenge.

or

1. Passive-constructive attention-getting, to

2. Passive-destructive attention-getting, to

3. Display of inadequacy.

The child may go through a passive demonstration of power and, sometimes, through a violent passivity revenge, *or* he may go through a passive-constructive attention-getting, to display of inadequacy.

To recognize which goal a child is using, the teacher should understand the meaning of the child's behavior. By using the accompanying tables in this chapter, teachers can become skilled in understanding the goals of children.

The younger the child, the easier it is to recognize his goal in any given situation. By the time a child reaches adolescence, he has learned to disguise his behavior so that the goals are not always obvious. Also, the adolescent has other mistaken goals, such as excitement, sex, drugs, etc. Up to the age of ten, the four mistaken goals prevail, but with corrective actions based on understanding and encouragement on the part of adults, the goals and the behavior of the children can change sometimes rapidly.

How can you, the teacher, diagnose these mistaken goals? Probably the most accurate clue to discovering the young child's goal is to observe your immediate response to the child's behavior. Your immediate response is in line with the child's expectations. Thus:

- If the teacher feels annoyed, it indicates Goal 1—attention-seeking.

- If the teacher feels defeated or threatened, it indicates Goal 2—power.

- If the teacher feels deeply hurt, it indicates Goal 3—revenge.

- If the teacher feels helpless, it indicates Goal 4—display of inadequacy.

Another indication is to observe the child's response to correction. If the child is seeking attention and gets it from the teacher, he will stop the misbehavior temporarily and then probably repeat it, or something similar. If he seeks power, he will refuse to stop the disturbance, or even increase it. If he seeks revenge, his response to the teacher's efforts to get him to stop will be to switch to some more violent action. A child using Goal 4 will not cooperate but will remain entirely passive and inactive.

Could It Be?

Once the teacher suspects which goal is motivating the child's misbehavior, it is important to clarify the goal (to confront it) with the child. The purpose of this confrontation is to confirm the goal and then to disclose it to the child. This psychological disclosure must be done in a friendly manner, without criticism, and never at the time of conflict. The emphasis is not on "why" but on "for what purpose." "Why" implies emphasis on the past, whereas "for what purpose" implies the child's intentions. Nothing can be done about the past, so a discussion about it is pointless and may also be inaccurate. However, the purpose in the child's present behavior can be determined, and she then has the opportunity to change her intentions. Intentions are plans for the future. She can, with guidance, take a different path.

An accurate disclosure of the child's present intentions produces a "recognition reflex" and the facial expression is a reliable indication of her goal, even though the child may say nothing or even says "no." Her mouth may say "no" while her nose says "yes." The recognition reflex is often a roguish smile, a twinkle of the eyes or the twitch of a facial muscle. Sometimes it is so open the child covers his face or bursts into laughter.

Confrontation Techniques

If you were the teacher or counselor, either in a classroom discussion period or in a private counseling situation, the conversation may go like this:

> *Teacher*—Do you know why you did (whatever the misbehavior was)?
>
> *Student*—No. (And at an aware-level he probably honestly means it).
>
> *Teacher*—Would you like to know? I have some ideas that may be helpful. Would you be willing to listen?
>
> *Student*—O.K. (Usually children will be interested.)
>
> *Teacher*—(In a non-judgmental and unemotional way, the teacher poses all the following four questions, but only one guess at a time.)

1. Could it be that you want special attention?
2. Could it be that you want your own way and hope to be boss?
3. Could it be that you want to hurt others as much as you feel hurt by them?
4. Could it be that you want to be left alone?

All four of these questions are always asked, sequentially, regardless of the child's answer or reflex because the child may be operating on more than one goal at a time. The teacher watches the body language as well as listening very carefully for the response, in order to catch the "recognition reflex." It is often a sudden change in the pupils of the eyes. Sometimes the confrontation itself helps the child to change. The next step is for the teacher to identify the goal accurately and to follow it up with the suggested corrective procedures. They may include using encouragement, logical consequences or finding a buddy in the same group.

Adler explains that it is not what happens to us but how we feel about it that is important. As pointed out before, all the goals of children's misbehavior are the result of the child's "faulty logic." His faulty private logic reflects his perception of reality.

By engaging the child in friendly conversation, by listening to his side of the story, the teacher may gain insights into ways he may help the child to correct his faulty interpretations and learn more suitable solutions. Class group discussions are also very helpful in correcting the child's faulty evaluation of situations. (See Chapter 13, "Typical Problems in the Classroom and Their Solutions.")

By not falling for the child's provocations, by use of logical and natural consequences rather than reward and punishment, by practicing mutual respect and by encouraging the child, a teacher can help him to overcome his mistaken goals and correct his behavior. Table 5.2, at the end of this chapter, is intended as a reference for helping you decide upon corrective procedures when facing a child with a behavior problem. First, observe the behavior and notice how frequently it occurs. Then, be sensitive to your own feelings or reactions to the behavior. Check yourself and do not say or do what you feel like doing; do something else. For example, you can extricate yourself from the conflict with the child. If the child throws a temper-tantrum, remove yourself, or him, from the scene, and do so quietly. Action is always more effective than words. You can also wait "quietly" until his outburst is over. It is impossible for an enraged child to listen to anybody. He usually displays temper for the benefit of an audience. If the audience disappears, the temper often disappears too.

Only later, during the next class discussion, should you confront him with his goals. In the meantime you will have an idea of the goal he is operating on (and it may be more than one) from observing his behavior and noting your own emotional reaction to it.

Use the advised method of confrontation by asking the four "Could it be... " questions and watch for the recognition reflex. When you are sure of the goal, use the suggested corrective procedures from the table. By patiently applying these methods you could see a rewarding improvement within a short time. Even though a recognition reflex may be noticed as a response to an early question, the teacher must proceed and ask all four questions, to make sure the child is not in more than one goal.

The most discouraged child can be trained by an informed teacher together with the support of a cooperative class. He can be encouraged to be happy and to learn enthusiastically, comfortable with the feeling that he really belongs to the group.

Table 5.1: Identifying the goals of children's misbehavior

| Increased social interest → | | Diminished social interest → | | |
| Useful and socially acceptable behavior | | Useless and socially unacceptable behavior | | |
Active constructive	Passive constructive	Active destructive	Passive destructive	Goals
Success	**Charm**	**Nuisance**	**Laziness**	**Goal 1: Attention getting**
Making cute remarks	Excessive pleasantness	The show-off	Bashfulness	Seeks proof of his approval or status (almost universal in preschool children)
Pursuing excellence for praise and recognition	"Model" child	The clown	Lack of ability	Will cease when reprimanded or given attention
Performing for recognition	Bright sayings	Walking question mark	Instability	
Performing stunts for attention	Exaggerated conscientiousness	"Enfant terrible"	Lack of stamina	
Being especially good	Excessive charm	Instability	Fearfulness	
Being industrious	"Southern Belle"	Acts "tough"	Speech impediments	
Being reliable	(These children are often "teacher's pets")	Makes minor mischief	Untidiness	
(May seem to be "ideal" student, but goal is self-elevation, not cooperation)			Self-indulgence	
			Frivolity	
			Anxiety	
			Eating difficulties	
			Performance difficulties	

		Goal 2: Power
A "Rebel"	**Stubborn**	Similar to destructive attention getting, but more intense
Argues	Laziness	Reprimand intensifies misbehavior
Contradicts	Disobedience	
Continues forbidden acts	Forgetting	
Temper-tantrums		
Bad habits		
Untruthfulness		
Dawdling		
		Goal 3: Revenge
Vicious	**Violent passivity**	Does things to hurt others
Stealing	Sullen	Makes self hated
Bed-wetting	Defiant	Retaliates
Violent and brutal (leader of juvenile delinquent gangs)		
		Goal 4: Display of inadequacy
	Hopeless	Assumes real or imagined deficiency to safeguard prestige
	Stupidity (pseudo feebleminded)	
	Indolence	
	Ineptitude	
	Inferiority complex	

The well-adjusted child has most of these qualities:

Respects the rights of others.
Is tolerant of others.
Is interested in others.
Cooperates with others.
Encourages others.
Is courageous.
Has a true sense of own worth.
Has a feeling of belonging.
Has socially acceptable goals.
Puts forth genuine effort.
Is willing to share rather than thinking, "How much can I get?"
Thinks in terms of "we" rather than "I."

This chart describes the behaviors of discouraged children up to ten years of age. Moving from Goals 4 to 3 (and so on) is a sign of improvement in the child's behavior.

Table 5.2: How to correct children's misbehavior

By interpretation of the four mistaken goals

Child's action and attitude	Teacher's reaction[*]	Ask these specific questions to diagnose[#]	Up to 10 years old Corrective procedure
Nuisance SHOW OFF CLOWN LAZY Puts others in his service, keeps teacher busy. Thinks, "Only when people pay attention to me do I have a place."	**Feels annoyed** GIVES SERVICE REMINDS OFTEN IS KEPT BUSY COAXES Thinks: "He occupies too much of my time" "I wish he would not bother me."	**Goal 1: Attention** A. "Could it be that you want me to notice you?" or B. "Could it be that you want me to do something special for you?"	**Never give attention when child demands it** Ignore the misbehaving child who is bidding for attention (punishing, nagging, giving service and advising are attention) Do not show annoyance. Be firm Give lots of attention at any other time
Stubborn ARGUES WANTS TO BE THE BOSS TEMPER TANTRUMS TELLS LIES DISOBEDIENT DOES THE OPPOSITE TO INSTRUCTIONS DOES LITTLE OR NO WORK Says, "If you don't let me do what I want, you don't love me." Thinks, "I only count if you do what I want."	**Feels defeated** TEACHER'S LEADERSHIP IS THREATENED Thinks: "He can't do this to me." "Who is running this class? He or I?" "He can't get away with this."	**Goal 2: Power** A. "Could it be that you want to show me that you can do what you want and no one can stop you?" or B. "Could it be that you want to be boss?"	**Don't fight—don't give in** Recognize and admit that the child has power Give power in situations where the child can use power productively Avoid power struggle Extricate yourself from the conflict Take your sails out of the wind Ask for his aid Respect the child Make agreement

Vicious STEALS SULLEN DEFIANT Will hurt animals, peers and adults. Tries to hurt as he feels hurt by others. Kicks, bites, scratches. Sore loser. Potential delinquent. Thinks, "My only hope is to get even with them."	**Feels deeply hurt** OUTRAGED DISLIKES CHILD RETALIATES (CONTINUAL CONFLICT) Thinks: "How can he be so mean?" "How can I get even with him?"	**Goal 3: Revenge** A. "Could it be that you want to hurt me and the pupils in the class?" or B. "Could it be that you want to get even?"	**Never say you are hurt** Don't behave as though you are hurt Apply natural consequences. (punishment produces more rebellion) Do the unexpected Persuade the child that he is liked Use group encouragement Enlist one buddy Try to convince him that he is liked
Feels hopeless "STUPID" ACTIONS INFERIORITY COMPLEX GIVES UP TRIES TO BE LEFT ALONE RARELY PARTICIPATES Says, "You can't do anything with me." Thinks, "I don't want anyone to know how inadequate I am."	**Feels helpless** THROWS UP HANDS DOESN'T KNOW WHAT TO DO Thinks: "I don't know what to do with him." "I give up." "I can't do anything with him."	**Goal 4: Display of inadequacy** A. "Could it be that you want to be left alone?" or B. "Could it be that you feel stupid and don't want people to know?"	**Encourage when the child makes mistakes** Make him feel worthwhile Show pleasure when he tries Say, "I do not give up along with you" Avoid support of inferior feelings Use a constructive approach Get class cooperation with pupil helpers Avoid discouragement yourself

* Teacher's reactions must not be expressed since the "natural" reaction in these circumstances will only reinforce the child's mistaken goal (except in goal 2).

All four questions must be asked of the child in this order even though the goal may be suspected. Do not change the wording.

NOTES

1. D. Dinkmeyer & R. Dreikurs, *Encouraging Children to Learn: The Encouragement Process* (Philadelphia: Brunner-Routledge, 2000), 58.

2. R. Dreikurs, *The Challenge of Parenthood* (New York: Hawthorn, 1948).

Chapter Six

The Teacher-Parent Conference

No one is in a better position to assist the parents in their difficult task than teachers who are familiar with effective methods of influencing children.

—**R. Dreikurs, *Psychology in the Classroom: A Manual for Teachers*, 2nd ed.**

Parents and teachers can help the child by their cooperation and mutual understanding. Many times it is advantageous for the conference between parents and teachers to occur in the child's home, because the teacher can observe the child's home setting and the kinds of interactions the child has with family members. However, regardless of where the conference takes place, the aim is that the teacher knows and understands

- the child's home situation
- family values
- the way that family members treat the child
- parental expectations
- the position the child holds in the family
- the child's relationships with siblings and friends

Knowing the home situation permits the teacher to help the parents resolve their difficulties with their children. Having the teacher and the parents talk together serves to unite the two areas of the child's life—her home and her school. This enables both to plan more effectively for the child than when the teacher and parent do not know whether they differ in their methods of treating the child. The more the two understand each other, the less the child will play school against home and vice versa. As a teacher, Pearl Cassel directed parent study groups at her home in order to help parents understand and correct misbehavior.

In talking with parents, teachers have many opportunities to learn indirectly a wide range of important information, such as general family attitudes, parents' views regarding discipline, whether the child has any responsibilities at home and, if so, whether she carries them out voluntarily or whether she has to be forced or coaxed. If the latter, how do the parents do it, and how much success do they have? Can the child be trusted to do her homework and develop her own time schedule? The child with the goal of contribution accepts responsibilities such as doing chores and homework. She does not need to be reminded. When the teacher and parent together work towards helping the child to be responsible, the child learns good work habits regarding chores and homework.

In the parent–teacher interview, the parents can learn from the teacher:

- about their child's behavior at school, and if the child has a mistaken goal, which it is and how the teacher uses corrective techniques
- the teacher's evaluation of the child
- the hopes and expectations the teacher has for the child
- the various rules the school has as well as those of the teacher (or those preferably made by the children in the class)
- the general program of the class.

Teachers should assure children that when they send a note home inviting the parents to the school, this does not contain "bad" information but is only an invitation for the parents to come to school. Children should be assured that parents are only invited to the school to make them happier, not to cause unpleasantness. Sometimes the student is also invited to be present for part of the discussion.

Before meeting with the parents, the teacher should jot down a tentative list of topics she may want to discuss, and prepare a few samples of the child's work including pictures, stories or a workbook. It is important that some of these samples deserve comments of worthwhile recognition. *Note:* If there is no such work available, then the teacher could relate an incident about the child that was helpful to the class—most children have some strength that can be related. The teacher should also tell the parents about something in which the child shows a particular interest, such as music, puzzles, watering the plants, running errands, helping other children or handing out papers.

The teacher may find a natural and engaging way to begin the interview. One way is to ask the parents how they feel about the child's progress at school. It is helpful to tell the parents what the purpose of the interview is: to share ideas and information that will best help the child.

At some time in the interview, the teacher should enquire how the parents feel about the classroom program as it pertains to the child, and what the parents feel toward the school itself. The teacher should seek specific information rather than general concerns.

Since the aim is to gain trust and mutual respect between parents and teacher, minimizing defensiveness is very important. If the parent makes negative comments about the school, rather than being defensive, the teacher might ask how the parent came to these conclusions.

If the child is unhappy at school, assess the possible reasons for this. For example, is the child unhappy whenever she cannot have her own way, or does the child want to stay at home with her mother or does the child feel inadequate at school?

Remember that the main purpose of the first meeting is to establish a relationship with the parents based on: (a) confidence and (b) the understanding that teacher and parents have a common goal—a happy, healthy, learning child.

Parents will participate more readily in a meeting if they are made to feel at ease and respected. The teacher who smiles and goes to greet the parents when they enter the conference area and shakes hands will find parents more open and trusting. Try not to have a desk positioned between you and the parents but, if you must have a desk, sit at one side, across a corner. Make sure both teachers' and parents' chairs are the same height. Sharing coffee or tea may be helpful in putting things at ease. If the parents do not speak English, an interpreter may be needed, which the school should be aware of and plan to have available.

Should a parent come to school angry, the teacher will be well advised to let the parent blow off steam before trying to respond to criticism. It is important to listen attentively—the teacher may glean some information that might indicate why the child is having a problem. Anger often fades away when it is met with a genuine wish to understand. Usually the parent calms down and then a quiet conversation can occur.

Parents who feel that the teacher is blaming them for the child's problem(s), either at home or at school, must be put at ease. Problem behavior can stem from many different causes.

If the child is experiencing difficulty with learning or shows misbehavior, the teacher should advise the parent of the following possible causes:

1. Does the child have trouble seeing the blackboard and doing close work? If so, advise that the child's sight be checked..

2. Can the child hear instructions? If not, advise that the child's hearing be checked.

3. Is the child's lack of learning due to hyperactivity? If so, advise that the lack of attention to tasks may be medical, and a medical checkup should be made.

A healthy child can learn well. The physical possibilities behind learning problems must be checked before considering what psychological interventions are appropriate.

Communication with parents is not always on a verbal level. People betray their feelings of anger, discouragement or discontent by a severity of tone in their voice, a critical look, a movement indicating impatience and other signs indicating antagonism. The teacher must be aware of such possibilities.

Issues Surrounding Homework

The teacher should reinforce with the parent that it is the child's responsibility to do his assigned homework by himself. Parents should be urged to monitor that the homework is being completed, but not actually contribute to the exercise unless specific information is requested by the child. Homework should not be an occasion for fights between the child and parents and should not be used as a weapon by either the child or the parent. Before assigning homework, teachers should win the cooperation of the students so they can look forward to completing the task with a sense of achievement.

Parents can help by

- providing a quiet place in which the child can work (they should avoid popping in every few minutes to see whether or not the child is doing the work)
- at times reading to or with the child to show encouragement (e.g., "You read a page and I'll read a page.")
- showing an interest in what the child is doing but not being overbearing.

Concluding the Parent–Teacher Interview

To wrap up the interview, the teacher can offer suggestions for the parents to use should the child misbehave at home (see below). An outline of subjects to be studied in class in the future can help the parents become more aware of what to expect in their child's progress. When they schedule a library visit or are viewing TV documentary programs, parents can steer the child in the appropriate direction. For instance, subjects such as famous people in history or identifying the planets in our universe may be on the agenda. The family discussion at home may then include references to these subjects. At closure of the interview, both teacher and parents will have learned more about the child and know they are working together for a common goal: a successful, confident and happy student.

Understanding Behavior in Children

Here are some recommendations for a teacher to offer parents, which will help them have a better understanding of their children's behavior. We will first consider a number of important issues that are helpful for parents to understand about behavior in children. Next, we'll discuss behavior in relationship to the four mistaken goals.

Children Want to Feel Belonging

A common complaint from parents is: "Our kids won't eat what is put in front of them, won't wear what we buy for them and refuse to sleep when we put them to bed. Why?"

Children want to have a sense of belonging. Kids who misbehave are discouraged and are struggling for significance. Deep down they are very often saying, "Hey look at me, I am around and I want to feel important." They are trying to find their place in the family but resort to negative behavior because they have not been given assurance of acceptance and a sense of self-worth.

Many children have not been taught how to cooperate and how to be helpful. From the wider culture that includes radio, TV, Internet or movies they have acquired a sense of equality, which they interpret as giving them permission for challenging and refuting their parents. When this sense of equality is part of the child's home and is accompanied by training for cooperation and mutual respect, the child interacts well with peers and adults. However, many children do not receive such training. In the past, children were trained in the home to be respectful to adults, to obey without question and to be seen and not heard. They usually found their place in the family by interacting with their brothers and sisters. They were given jobs to do that contributed to the survival of the whole family. They felt needed. However, they also were controlled by punishment and reward. That autocratic system, supported by province or state, church and school, controlled children for thousands of years.

Today, many families do not function according to these traditional rules, and parents are painfully experiencing the changing styles of a rapidly evolving society that has become politically democratic without teaching the necessary skills for democratic parenting. What is the answer? To counteract the autocratic traditions, professional and popular articles and books advocated what might be called the "Do your own thing" philosophy. This told parents that infants were entitled to satisfaction upon demand. Efforts were made to create child-centered homes. The unfortunate consequence of this approach was that in many cases the former domination by the adults was replaced by tyranny of the children. Instead of the parents behaving as if they were in the position of superiority, the children behaved in this way and their parents became their servants. Many parents were led to believe that their children, like flowers, would grow into loving cultured human beings if they indulged them and imposed no restraints. Those same parents are now dismayed to find that their teenagers have not blossomed as flowers but have become uncontrollable weeds.

That method did not work. What now? How can we cope with our kids today? Children and parents of today live in a democracy with a sense of equality. Because neither indulgence nor autocratic control is effective, the following points are important for parents to remember:

1. Respect the child and yourself.
2. Build on strengths and rarely talk or nag about weaknesses.
3. Remember that a child needs encouragement like a plant needs light and water.

4. Take time for training. It is time well spent and prevents bigger problems later.

5. Avoid talking to the back of a child's head or shouting directions or reprimands at him from a different room.

6. Speak and listen to your child with complete attention, including physical closeness and eye contact.

7. Tell him what to do only once. It is an insult to the child to repeat it.

8. Remember it is the quality of time that we spend with a child that counts. When both parents are working or a single parent is trying to cope, remember that there is no need to feel guilty.

9. One hour of loving and sharing time spent each day with your child is worth hundreds of hours of poor quality experiences. This hour belongs to your child. Turn off your cell phone, turn off the TV and give of yourself whole heartedly. Let your child choose the activity or topic of conversation. It may be a game like dominoes, Scrabble or chess, or the child might want to go for a walk or to the park, museum or zoo. It may be to shoot hoops or kick around a soccer ball. It may be cooking something together for the family to enjoy. It may involve some help on a school project, some shared reading or preparing a card, letter or gift for a relative or friend. It might also be some basic training in life skills.

10. Set up family council meetings for one hour each week—maybe after Sunday dinner, even though you may have only one child and no partner. Two can become a group. Discuss the good things that have happened in the previous week. Plan the menus and chore distributions for the following week. Solve individual problems by participation in decision-making. Develop family rules; then write them down on a chart or card and post them on the fridge or near the entrance door. Decide as a family what the natural or logical consequences will be if the rules are

broken. Re-evaluate the progress of all family members at the next weekly meeting.

11. Trust your child but give guidance to build in probable success. Show your love and faith in your child's ability to learn and grow. Don't hide them.

12. Remember, we teach responsibility by giving responsibility. Children learn more from a model than from a critic. As well as watching your child's behavior, watch your own.

13. If you take your child to a restaurant or a friend's house, please take some hand toys or quiet games that will amuse her while you are visiting.

If the parents feel the child is misbehaving, here are some thoughts you could offer:

1. Act—but refrain from talking because that will only reinforce the misbehavior, not correct it. If the child has a temper tantrum, remember that he cannot hear what you say.

2. Accept the child but not the disruptive behavior. Separate the deed from the doer.

3. Be consistent. If you have set limits, stick to them. If you say "No," mean it, and don't change your mind.

4. Be firm but kind. State what you mean and say it only once but with a firm and friendly voice.

5. Apply the natural or logical consequences without emotion. Never say, "I told you so."

6. Refrain from nagging or scolding. It may also reinforce that child's mistaken concept of how to get special attention.

7. If you find yourself losing control and wanting to hit your child, find alternatives. Hitting is not the way to help the child. If this experience happens often, please get help by seeing your doctor, agencies, clinics or other professional community resources that provide services to families and children in your local area.

8. If the child's behavior is serious enough to affect the family functions or the school or requires the intervention of the police, deal with the situation as objectively as possible and do what needs to be done without subjectively feeling overly guilty. You cannot take full blame for your child's mistakes. He must take responsibility and learn that certain infractions result in certain consequences. Don't deny him the opportunity to grow through experience.

9. Don't side with your child against other adults, neighbors, school teachers or policemen. They probably want to help you and your child.

10. Keep in mind your long-range goal—to help your child to become responsible and happy—to help him to grow into a loving, competent, independent adult.

Understand the Four Mistaken Goals and How to Cope with Misbehavior

Children naturally want to feel a sense of belonging to their family and their school. They need to feel significant; they want to be helpful. They like a feeling of accomplishment—to be able to do things for themselves. They need our love, acceptance, patience and encouragement in their struggle to grow up.

A well-behaved child cooperates because he feels encouraged. A misbehaving child is a discouraged child.

When a child under the age of ten misbehaves, he is trying to claim self-worth in a way that is in response to his own faulty private motivational logic. He may be misbehaving in line with one of the following four mistaken goals that he believes will give him a feeling of significance.

1. He may be seeking undue attention and saying to himself, "I only count when adults give me special attention." In order to correct this behavior, try the following:

   • Ignore the attention-seeking behavior unless it hurts others or is damaging property.

- Be firm but do not show annoyance because that will only reinforce the mistaken goal.
- Give lots of attention only when the child is being cooperative. Catch a kid doing something good.

2. A child may become more discouraged and resort to power struggles. She may say to herself, "I only count when I am the boss and you do what I want." She may even say to you, "If you don't let me do what I want, then you don't love me." This is emotional bribery. Don't fall for it!

In order to return to a harmonious relationship, try the following:

- Try to avoid power struggles. If your child provokes you, refuse to enter the battle, recognizing that it takes two to fight and you have the maturity to refuse and even go to another room if you need to get away from your child and reduce the emotional stress of the situation.

- Recognize and admit to the child that she has power, and steer her into using it constructively rather than inviting her to defeat you.

- Respect the child but maintain your own dignity.

3. The more discouraged child may be revengeful. He will be sullen, defiant and vicious. He destroys things and hurts people. He is a potential delinquent. He thinks, "My only hope is to hurt and get even." How can you help him?

- Never say or imply that you are hurt by his misbehavior, because that will only reinforce his mistaken goal—that he can indeed cause you and others pain and thus satisfy his vengeance.

- Show and tell the child how he can be liked.

- Do the unexpected and allow natural consequences to teach him through experience.

4. The most discouraged child is one who is withdrawn and has given up trying to succeed and be acceptable. She is passive and quiet, a poor learner at school and probably friendless. She is saying to herself at an unconscious level, "I don't want anyone to know how inadequate I feel, so leave me alone because you can't do anything with me." To help her, you will need personal strength and encouragement from others. Try the following:

- Work with the child to help her feel worthwhile.

- Acknowledge whatever effort the child makes. Remember that the quality of the product is not as important as the fact that the child expends effort.

- Encourage her to make friends, give her your undivided, loving attention for about an hour each day; then take time to relax and refresh yourself. Don't get caught up in her discouragement. She needs strong positive support. She does not need pity because that will give her permission to feel sorry for herself.

Remember, nobody is more miserable than someone who wallows in self-pity.

The above are suggestions to help you become a happier, more competent and more confident parent. In addition to these important points, however, do not overlook the possibility that the misbehavior may be related to a physical illness. The child may have allergies to certain foods. His ears may be infected, or his eyes may be deficient, and that may be the underlying problem. His teeth may hurt. As a parent, your first action is to check with your child's doctor and dentist. Keep your child's teacher informed of your concerns. Discuss with his teacher the possible solutions. Don't try to do it alone. Help is available and many parents, like you, are struggling with this increasingly difficult job of child training.

Life for you and your child can be beautiful, successful and rewarding. ACT NOW!

If you would like to have more information in dealing with a particular problem, contact your local community resources for family and children's services.

A Message from Every Child in the Class

1. Don't spoil me. I know quite well that I ought not to have all I ask for. I'm only testing you.

2. Don't be afraid to be firm with me. I prefer it. It lets me know where I stand.

3. Don't use force with me. It teaches me that power is all that counts. I will respond more readily to being led.

4. Don't be inconsistent. That confuses me and makes me try harder to get away with everything that I can.

5. Don't make promises; you may not be able to keep them. That will discourage my trust in you.

6. Don't fall for my provocations when I do and say things just to upset you. Then I'll try for more such "victories."

7. Don't be too upset when I say, "I hate you." I don't mean it, but I want you to feel sorry for what you have done to me.

8. Don't make me feel smaller than I am. I will make up for it by behaving like a "big shot."

9. Don't do things for me that I can do for myself. It makes me feel like a baby, and I may continue to put you in my service.

10. Don't let my "bad habits" get me a lot of your attention. It only encourages me to continue them.

11. Don't correct me in front of people. I'll take much more notice if you talk quietly with me in private.

12. Don't try to preach to me. You'd be surprised how well I know what's right and wrong.

13. Don't make me feel that my mistakes are sins. I have to learn to make mistakes without feeling that I am a bad person or a failure.

14. Don't nag. If you do, I shall have to protect myself by appearing deaf.

15. Don't demand explanations for my wrong behavior. I really don't know why I did it.

16. Don't tax my honesty too much. I am easily frightened into telling lies.

17. Don't forget that I love to experiment. I learn from it so please put up with it.

18. Don't protect me from consequences; I need to learn from experience.

19. Don't take too much notice of my small ailments. I may learn to enjoy poor health if it gets me too much attention.

20. Don't put me off when I ask *honest* questions. If you do, you will find that I stop asking and seek my information elsewhere.

21. Don't answer "silly" or meaningless questions. I just want you to keep busy with me.

22. Don't ever think that it is beneath your dignity to apologize to me. An honest apology makes me feel surprisingly warm toward you.

23. Don't ever suggest that you are perfect or infallible. It gives you and me too much to live up to.

24. Don't worry about the little amount of time we spend together. It is how we spend it that counts.

25. Don't let my fears arouse your anxiety. Then I will become more afraid. Show me courage.

26. Don't forget that I can't thrive without lots of understanding and encouragement, but I don't need to tell you that, do I?

27. Treat me the way you treat your friends; then I will be your friend, too.

28. Remember, I learn more from a model than a critic.

Chapter Seven

Competition in an Elementary School

In an atmosphere of competition no one child can be sure of his place in the group.

—R. Dreikurs, *Psychology in the Classroom:*
A Manual for Teachers, **2nd ed.**

You might ask, "Why should we not promote competition in our elementary classrooms? Competition is the way of the world. Why shelter our children from the reality of modern life?"

Many parents want our schools to train children in competitive living because they believe that such training is necessary to prepare a young person to enter the competitive corporate culture. These parents do not understand that competition for marks, grades, treats or prizes only divides a class into two camps. The smaller camp is comprised of children who come to feel superior and look down on the larger group who feel inferior.

In a competitive elementary school children are not willing to cooperate and they do not respect each other for their individual intrinsic worth or basic human dignity. Such children do not learn to meet the needs of a situation or to contribute with a healthy desire to be helpful. They do not feel that they are worthwhile because they don't feel part of the group. Their philosophy of life is, "If you can't join 'em—beat 'em!" Schoolyard bullies and haughty children have these faulty ideas of how to feel significant.

Only for the few with above-average abilities is it possible for competition to be a rewarding experience. Even for bright and talented children, competition may be far from enjoyable, because in spite of frequent occasions for "winning" or being successful, the threat of failure and losing is at best unpleasant and, more often, brings painful stresses and anxieties. For the majority of children, who do not ordinarily "win" and many times are not successful in their accomplishments, competition provides constant feelings of inadequacy and is the most discouraging method of motivating learning. Such children give up and regress instead of making progress. Knowing they can't "win," they become disengaged from the teacher and falter in their learning.

As long as the competitive spirit is fostered, a child will waste his energies thinking about winning or losing, which will sap his strength and potential for the task at hand. When children in school are trained to be competitive, they invariably exert effort only when they win. When they lose, they blame others or themselves and often withdraw from activities, because the fear of losing is highly charged with negative emotions. Instead of focusing on learning and on improvement, such competitively trained children often get very discouraged and withdraw from utilizing their potential and strengths.

A person, adult or child, who was taught without competition, can function better in a competitive society because she is not concerned with what the others are doing but with what she is doing herself. This means she is free to be concerned with others as friends, neighbors and fellow human beings, rather than as competitors. This noncompetitive person is not hung up with feelings of superiority or inferiority, status, prejudice or intolerance. Since she really respects herself, she can treat everyone with equal mutual respect. She can live and let live without criticizing other people's attitudes or behavior. She has the courage to be imperfect.

We cannot make a child learn or behave for long with competition. If we teach her in a democratic environment, we can gain her cooperation and influence her for a far longer period.

Alfred Adler wrote at the beginning of the 20th century about the destructive effects of competition. His ideas are still revolutionary in many respects, as much as they were when he first wrote them. He pointed out that only when children and adults have learned cooperation, and have learned concern for the welfare of others as much as they have learned concern for their own welfare, will they be prepared for the challenges that life brings. In contrast, competition leads individuals to try to best others, to be concerned only with their own success, and not to strive to contribute and help. This leads to tragic consequences for the group and for the individual.

When children learn competition and not cooperation, only a few can "win" and feel confident while the large majority feels defeated and discouraged. Only cooperation and social interest can bring about lasting improvement in morale and enjoyment of life. Adlerians have seen many "difficult" and discouraged children become effective and happy at home and in the classroom when they experience cooperation and belonging in the family and at school. Such a feeling of belonging requires cooperation, not competition. It requires people helping each other, cheering each other on for putting out effort, encouraging each other, and emphasizing the gains of all members rather than focusing on the failures of most and the successes of a few.

Modern society has values that serve to discourage many persons. When the child fails at a task, instead of helping the child to gain in skill and confidence, adults tend to demean or punish the child. Over-ambitious parents create a double dose of discouragement when the child brings home a poor report card: The child feels humiliated at school and then is doubly scolded and demeaned at home. If a teacher understands this sorry state, the teacher is in a wonderful position to help offset this downward spiral.

The teacher can help the child learn that others are not his enemy, that failure is not the inevitable path of his life. By encouraging and befriending the child, by soliciting the class to help the child believe he is valuable and effective, the teacher can create a long-term benefit for the child. Moreover, such encouragement and cooperation provides a model for the child, who will thereby also learn to help others and to contribute to their well-being.

Teachers who use the methods of cooperation rather than competition, of uniting a class rather than putting the children into opposition of winners and losers, can bring about unbelievable improvements in all their students. Whenever you use the democratic approach with students, rather than the competitive one, you will be amazed and delighted by the spirit of cooperation and helpfulness you receive.

In the Hall-Dennis report, _Living and Learning_, published by the Ontario government in 1967, the authors state:

> Each and every child has the right to learn, to play, to laugh, to dream, to love, to dissent, to reach upward, and to be himself. Our children need to be treated as human beings—exquisite, complex, and elegant in their diversity. They must be made to feel that the world is waiting for their sunrise, and that their education heralds the rebirth of an "Age of Wonder." Then, surely, the children of tomorrow will be more flexible, more adventurous, more daring and courageous than we are, and better equipped to search for truth, each in his own way.

Chapter Eight

Encouragement
in the Classroom

*A child needs encouragement like a plant needs sun and
water. Unfortunately, those who need encouragement
most get it the least because they behave in such a way
that our reaction to them pushes them further into
discouragement and rebellion.*

—R. Dreikurs

The goal of encouragement is to increase the child's confidence in
himself and to convey to him that he is good enough *as he is*—not
just *as he might be*. Only when parents and teachers are encouraging does a child develop courage. Encouragement produces courage.
Undefeatable courage is the courage to be imperfect.

Too many children, and adults too, waste their potential by
trying to be perfect, by thinking about how good they are or
conversely how inadequate they are—whether they are going to
succeed or fail. It is only when such thoughts are completely
discarded that we can utilize our energies to meet the needs of the
situation and cope with the problems that face us.

The desire to be perfect makes spontaneity and creativity
almost impossible because the child may fear the danger of making
a mistake. How can the teacher acquire the necessary courage to be
imperfect if she, in her daily routine, constantly has to watch for
every infraction of perfection?

It may be a good strategy for a teacher to deliberately make a mistake (e.g., the wrong date on the blackboard) then demonstrate, with a brief apology to the class, that we all err from time to time.

As teachers we can build up the strengths of each pupil. We should mark only correct responses instead of focusing on mistakes; then we can use those mistakes as a positive learning motivation and not as a critical evaluation of the child. If we want to find the reason for a child's making a mistake, or for understanding his wrong concept and assumptions, avoid criticism. Only when we learn his true motives can we start to help him correct his misbehavior.

We can increase every child's sense of worth if we appreciate his effort or opinion and avoid "putting him down." To offer this encouragement requires constant observation of the pupil's reactions. It is more than a single action. It expresses a whole process of interactions.

Encouragement is not what one says and does but how one does it. It is directed toward increasing the child's belief in himself. The more one has faith in a child, the more one can see the good in him as he is, the more does one encourage.

Children who have little self-esteem develop a defeatist attitude, and give up when faced with anything difficult or puzzling to them. In an atmosphere where there is freedom and encouragement to think, combined with respect for one another, a child's confidence grows and, with it, his ability to think creatively.

Until we learn to recognize discouragement as soon as it occurs, and develop skills to help the child overcome it, we will continue to raise children who are more or less demoralized, regardless of the achievements they may have to their credit.

The moment discouragement sets in, the child's personality changes. Regardless of how limited the onset of discouragement may be, it affects the child's self-evaluation, diminishes his self-respect, renders him vulnerable, and makes him timid and fearful. We need courage to meet the tasks of life and to fulfill our potential. Discouragement drains a person's strength and courage.

No child would switch to the socially unacceptable side of life if he were not discouraged. When a child believes that he has no place in the group and can't succeed with useful means, he will engage in misbehavior and become a negative influence in the classroom. This furthers his discouragement and creates a vicious circle. Democratic teachers have the means and the courage to break that vicious circle.

When we encourage children they feel free to learn and create. When we discourage children, we suppress the desire to learn and the joy it brings. In a memorable passage, Albert Einstein explained why he was unable to think about scientific problems for a year after his final exams. He wrote, "It is in fact nothing short of a miracle that the modern methods of instruction have not yet entirely strangled the holy curiosity of inquiry. It is a very grave mistake to think that the enjoyment of seeing and searching can be promoted by means of coercion and a sense of duty."

Yet, life and joy cannot be easily subdued. The blade of grass shatters the concrete. The spring flowers bloom in Hiroshima. An Einstein emerges from the academies. Those who would reduce, control and suppress must lose in the end because the ecstatic forces of life, growth and change are too numerous, too various and too tumultuous.

To nurture these ecstatic forces of life we may use some of the following 20 points to encourage every student who looks to us for guidance:

1. Avoid discouraging your students, because the feelings of inferiority that all humans experience in one form or another must be overcome if we are to function well.

2. Work for improvement, not perfection.

3. Commend effort. *Effort is very significant, especially for the discouraged child.*

4. Separate the deed from the doer: One may reject the child's actions without rejecting the child.

5. Build on strengths, not on weaknesses. A misbehaving child has the power to defeat the adult. Give him credit for this.

6. Show your faith in the child. This must be sincere, so one must first learn to trust the child.

7. Mistakes should not be viewed as failures. We need to take away the stigma of failure. Failure usually indicates lack of skill. One's worth is not dependent on success.

8. Failure and defeat will only stimulate special effort when there remains the hope of eventual success. They do not stimulate a deeply discouraged child who has lost all hope of succeeding.

9. Stimulate and lead the child, but do not try to push him ahead. Let him move at his own speed.

10. Remember that genuine happiness comes from self-confidence; children need to learn to take care of themselves, and the more confidence they have in themselves, the more they can do this.

11. Integrate the child into the group. Treating the child as "something special" increases his over-ambition. An over-ambitious child who cannot succeed usually switches to the useless side of life with the "private logic": "If I can't be best, I'll at least be the worst." Even more serious, he may give up altogether.

12. Stimulating competition usually does not encourage children. Those who see hope of winning may put forth extra effort, but the stress is on winning rather than on cooperation and contribution. The less competitive one is, the better one is able to withstand competition—in childhood as well as later in life.

13. Praise is not the same as encouragement. Praise may have an encouraging effect at some times, but it often discourages and causes anxiety and fear. Some come to depend on praise and will perform only for recognition in ever-increasing amounts. Success accompanied by special praise for the result may make the child fear "I can never do it again!"

14. Success is a by-product. Preoccupation with the obligation to succeed is intimidating and the resulting fear and anxiety often contribute to failure. If one functions with the emphasis on what contribution one may make or how one may cooperate with others, success usually results.

15. Help the child develop the courage to be imperfect. We should learn from our mistakes and take them in our stride.

16. Don't give responsibility and significance only to those who are already responsible. Giving opportunities to be responsible to a child who is discouraged may make it worthwhile for him to cooperate. Freedom with responsibility is actually taught by this method.

17. Solicit the help of other members of the class to help a discouraged child find his place in useful ways.

18. Remember that discouragement is contagious. A discouraged child tends to discourage his teacher.

19. Avoid trying to mend your own threatened ego by discouraging others or by looking down on them. This neurotic control is damaging to all in society, but visibly worse in the teaching profession. As an adult, with greater knowledge and power than your students, you steadfastly avoid enhancing your ego at the expense of children who, inevitably, have less skill and knowledge.

20. Overcome your own pessimism and develop an optimistic approach to life. Optimism is contagious—it not only encourages you, but those around you.

Many teachers feel that encouragement is the same as praise. This is not true. The difference between the two is subtle but very important. The effect on the child is very different between praise and encouragement. Praise provides external sources of motivation, and the child needs to develop inner sources of motivation. Praise should not be the way to stimulate children into appropriate or effective behavior. Internal motivation comes from the child's own sense of satisfaction of doing a job well. This inner motivation is what the child needs.

The remarks "Well done!" or "Keep up the good work" are effective. We must remember, also, that perfection is an illusory goal. Striving for perfection sometimes has merit but many times leads to unnecessary discouragement and feelings of inadequacy, because perfection is so rarely attained. Whatever we do or say, we must be careful never to imply that the child's personal worth depends only on his accuracy.

Encouragement is needed by all children, particularly when they make mistakes. Encouragement is often difficult for the adult to express, and it takes practice. If we watch a child closely when he is receiving praise, we may discover some astonishing facts. Some children gloat, some panic, some express, "So what?" and some seem to say, "Well, finally!" We are suddenly confronted with the fact that we need to see how the child interprets what is going on rather than assume that he regards everything as we do.

Examination of the intention of the praiser shows that he is offering a reward. "If you are good you will have the reward of being high in my esteem." What is wrong with this approach? Why not help the child learn to do the right thing by earning a high place in a teacher's esteem? If we look at the situation from the child's point of view, we will find the mistake of this approach. How does praise affect the child's self-image? He may get the impression that his personal worth depends upon how he measures up to the demands and values of others. "If I am praised, my personal worth is high. If I am scolded, I am bad. If I am ignored, I am worthless."

When this child becomes an adult, his effectiveness, his ability to function, his capacity to cope with life's tasks, will depend entirely upon his estimation of how he stands in the opinion of others. He will live constantly on an elevator of happiness—up and down, frequently with someone else pushing the button. Praise is apt to center the attention of the child upon himself. He will say, "How do I measure up?" rather than "What does this situation need?" This gives rise to a fictive-goal of "self-being-praised" instead of the reality-goal of "what-can-I-do-to-help?"

Another child may come to see praise as his right. Therefore, life is unfair if he doesn't receive praise for every effort. "Poor me—no one appreciates me." Or, he may feel no obligation to perform if no praise is forthcoming. "What's in it for me? What will I get out of it? If no praise (reward) is forthcoming, why should I bother?" Praise can be terribly discouraging. If the child's efforts fail to bring the desired amount of praise he may assume either that he isn't good enough or that what he has to offer isn't worth the effort, so he gives up.

If a child has set exceedingly high standards for himself, praise may sound like mockery or scorn, especially when his efforts fail to measure up to his own standards. In such a child, praise only serves to increase his anger with himself and his resentment at others for not understanding his dilemma.

In all our efforts to encourage children, we must be alert to the child's response. The accent must move from "You are good" to "How you have helped in the total situation." Anything we do that reinforces a child's false image of himself is discouraging. Whatever we do that helps a child see that he is an important part of a functioning unit—that he can contribute, cooperate, participate within the total situation—is encouragement. We must learn to see that as he is, the child is acceptable, even though his work may not be.

Praise may be intended by the person giving the praise as a reward for accomplishment, but the child interprets the praise in terms of himself as a person. The praise threatens the child's self-confidence. "What if I don't do well next time and do not get praised?" Praise should never be used to refer to the child as a person, like the statement "You are a good boy." Lack of praise then implies being a "bad boy."

Praise tends to fasten attention upon the individual. Little satisfaction or self-fulfillment comes from this direction. Encouragement stimulates one's effort and fastens attention upon one's capacity to join and contribute to humanity. Encouragement helps us to be aware of our inner strength and ability to cope.

Praise focuses on the child; encouragement focuses on the task. Praise leads to self-serving and self-elevating striving; encouragement leads to contribution and cooperation.

The following chart stresses this crucial difference between praise and encouragement. The sentences under praise are not encouraging but produce a false superior self-awareness.

Praise	Encouragement
Aren't you wonderful	Isn't it nice that you can help? to be able to do this!
	We appreciate your help.
	How tidy our classroom looks now!
	Thanks for comforting Jerome. It was a big help.
	I like your drawing. The colors are so pretty together.
	How much neater your desk looks now that your books are put away.
	How nice that you could figure that out for yourself.
	Your skill is growing!
I'm so proud of you for getting good grades. (You are high in my esteem.)	I'm so glad you enjoy learning (adding to your own resources.)
I'm proud of you for being so nice on the school bus.	We all enjoyed being together on the school bus.
I'm awfully proud of your performance in the recital.	It is good to see how much you enjoy playing your instrument.
	We all appreciate the job you did. I give you credit for working hard.

As we work with children, we very quickly learn that our voice can be of major importance. We can say the same sentence in an encouraging or discouraging way, depending on the tone, timbre and other ways we communicate our warmth or disdain, our approval or rejecting attitude, to the child or class.

The following remarks are suggestions that will be encouraging to a child, but they will work only if you express a feeling of trust, confidence, acceptance and belief in that child. If you express a feeling of moralizing, preaching or impatience, these same suggestions will have discouraging results. (The idea is to catch a child "doing something good" whenever you can.)

1. "You're doing a good job of..."

    Children should be encouraged when they do not expect it, when they are not asking for it. It is possible to point out some useful act or contribution in each child. Even a comment about something small and insignificant to us may have great importance to a child.

2. "You are improving in..."

    Growth and improvement is something we should expect from all children. They may not be where we would like them to be, but if there is progress, there is less chance for discouragement. If they can see some improvement, children will usually continue to try.

3. "We like (enjoy) you, but we don't like what you do..."

    After a child makes a mistake or misbehaves, he often feels he is not liked. A child should never think he is not liked. It is important to distinguish between the child and his behavior, between the act and the actor.

4. "You can help me (us, the others, etc.) by..."

    To feel useful and helpful is important to everyone. Children want to be helpful: we have to give them the opportunity.

5. "Let's try it together..."

    Children who think they have to do things perfectly are often afraid to attempt something alone or new, for fear of making a mistake or failing. They are likely to feel more secure with a group project.

6. "So you made a mistake? Now, what can you learn from your mistake?"

    Mistakes are an inevitable part of learning. The very notion of "learning" implies that what one did previously is not as effective as what one is doing at this time. Learning implies that we improve. If we say we learn to play the piano, that means we made mistakes previously that we are not making now. Perfection may happen, but only after, not during, one's learning. We cannot undo what has already occurred, but we can improve on it or fix it. We can always do something different in the future. Mistakes can teach the child a great deal, and he will learn if he is not made to feel embarrassed for having made a mistake.

7. "You would like us to think you can't do it, but we think you can..."

   This approach could be used when the child says or conveys that something is too difficult for him. If he tries and fails, he has at least had the courage to try. Our expectations should be consistent with the child's ability and maturity.

8. "Keep trying. Don't give up..."

   When a child is trying, but not meeting much success, a comment like this might be helpful.

9. "I'm sure you can straighten this out (solve this problem, etc.), but if you need any help, you know where to find me..."

   Teachers need to express confidence that children are able to resolve their own conflicts.

10. "I can understand how you feel (not sympathy; but empathy) but I'm sure you'll be able to handle it..."

    Sympathizing with another person seldom helps him; rather it conveys that life has been unfair to him. Understanding the situation (empathizing) and believing in the child's ability to adjust to it is of much greater help.

All that has been suggested in this chapter is crucial to the intricate process of education. Success breeds fulfillment, self-acceptance and the belief that one can achieve. Frustration and discouragement lead to suppressed aggression or to aggressive action, conflict and deviant behavior. It is only when the child understands himself, his needs, purposes and attitudes and develops an awareness of how to relate to others that he is freed to become involved in the educative process.

This process can be idealized in the following philosophy:

What Learning Could Be Like

To learn joyously and enthusiastically.

To learn cooperation for the well-being of society.

To learn discipline by stimulation from within.

To learn responsibility by being given responsibility.

To learn empathy for others by becoming sensitive to them.

To learn a sense of security that comes from the faith that we can cope with the insecurity of life.

To learn self-esteem by living without shame or guilt.

To learn to like oneself, by feeling accepted as one is.

To learn to love and grow by living with friendship and acceptance.

To learn commonly agreed upon knowledge and skills of the ongoing culture.

To learn to reason and make decisions by participating in decision-making.

To learn appreciation by respecting the contribution each person makes.

To learn confidence by living with encouragement.

Chapter Nine

Use Logical Consequences, Not Punishment

> *Punishment...is only effective with children who do not need it, with whom one could reason. Those the teacher wishes to impress with punishment, shrug it off as part of the fortune of war.*
>
> **—R. Dreikurs, *Psychology in the Classroom: A Manual for Teachers*, 2nd ed.**

When the teacher punishes, the child's reaction is, "If the teacher has the right to punish me, I have the same right to punish her." This is the primary reason why our classrooms are filled with acts of retaliation. Yet many teachers still expect positive results from a method that at best brings temporary compliance. Punishment represents an autocratic method for exerting control, which does not fit into the democratic society of today.

In the 19th century Herbert Spencer, a renowned English philosopher, pointed to the ineffectiveness of punishment in a democratic setting and distinguished between punishment and natural consequences. In the 20th century Jean Piaget, a well-known Swiss developmental psychologist, extended this concept by distinguishing between retributive justice, which is punishment, and distributive justice, which is the power and force of reality and of the social group.

You may believe that reward and punishment are essential for the rearing and teaching of children. Many share that belief. But, reward and punishment have detrimental effects on the development of the child, particularly in the democratic atmosphere that prevails today. Only in an autocratic society are they an effective and necessary means of obtaining conformity; they presuppose that certain persons are endowed with superior authority and that as superiors they are entitled to exert control over inferior persons. In a democracy, social equality is granted to everybody, and the punitive power of some persons over others is refuted. Many people, however, still have difficulty accepting the democratic approach at home, in the classroom and in the workplace.

In a democratic atmosphere the control of parents and teachers over children diminishes. Outside pressures on the child can no longer "make" the child perform. The child reacts to rewards by regarding them as his right, refusing to do his share unless he gets one. Conversely, if the child is punished, he feels that he has the same right to punish the adults.

If you want to influence the development of children you will find that the methods suggested in this book fit into the new democratic era. First, the principle of reward and punishment must be abandoned. This does not mean embracing a permissive attitude. Permissiveness tends to lead to chaos and anarchy. Instead, choose democratic methods that are based on the recognition of mutual equality, mutual respect and order in the classroom.

In a system of mutual respect a job is done because it needs doing and the satisfaction comes from the harmony of two or more people doing a job together. Children don't need bribes to be good. They actually *want* to be good. Good behavior by children springs from their desire to belong, to contribute usefully and to cooperate. When we bribe a child for her good behavior we are, in effect, showing her that we do not trust her, which is a form of discouragement. The system of rewarding children for good behavior is as detrimental as the system of punishment. There is no reward that totally satisfies. True satisfaction comes from a sense of contribution and participation. Children who are trained to be competitive only feel worthwhile when they are on top or superior. If they don't "win," they feel unhappy and inferior. Children trained in an atmosphere of cooperation know that by merely existing they are an accepted part of humanity.

Some teachers believe that, without punishment, or threat of it, children will not conform or perform. In the past, some even said that the only way of maintaining discipline was by using corporal punishment. But our present society and boards of education have outlawed that approach. Thus, some teachers who have relied on the use of corporal punishment in the past feel stymied and are groping for new methods. As part of our search for ways of dealing with children, codes of conduct have come to exist in schools, clubs and summer camps, and on school buses—wherever children come together as a group.

All recent research in education and child–adult relationships finds that punishment is, at best, only a temporary deterrent to repeated misbehavior. (In Behavior Modification, the reward is a temporary crutch.) The teacher who does the punishing may feel a sense of satisfaction himself, but as a training device, the actual punishment is useless. You may ask, "How can I train a child without the threat of punishment?"

The most effective training devices are an outcome of the understanding that human beings are basically cooperative—not competitive. Alfred Adler explained early in the 20th century that humans working together has led to art, music, science, and the utilization of the full potential of all individuals. Humans individually are relatively small and weak when compared to speedy or mighty non-human animals; by working together in cooperation, humans are able to survive and to develop and to reach great accomplishments.

The democratic teacher will use natural and logical consequences but not punishment. Punishment invites retaliation and is not an effective teaching method. Logical consequences are structured by the adult and, whenever possible, arranged in advance through discussion with the child; they must be experienced by the child as logical in nature. If the child does not consider it logical, she will interpret it as punishment and thus this method needs to be used with skill, caution and understanding. If she does see it as logical, she will see the consequence of her behavior by experience and will learn from it. However, logical consequences should never be used in a power struggle—they inevitably backfire.

Natural consequences are based on the natural flow of events and are those that take place without adult interference or even adult involvement. They are called "natural" because the outcome following a given behavior is a function of "reality" (and in that sense "nature"). When an adult forgets to take an umbrella to go shopping on a day that the weather forecaster predicted rain, and the adult consequently gets very wet, this is an example of "natural consequences." All of us experience them throughout our daily life. These are the best training techniques.

The following are some of the reasons for using logical and natural consequence:

We want to convey to the child that she is able to take care of her problem, not that she must do what we decide.

We should not take away responsibilities from children nor should we, rather than the children themselves, experience the consequences of their actions.

We have no right to impose our wills on children. However, we do have an obligation to guide, and we have an obligation not to give in to children's undue demands.

We have no *right*, in a democratic society, to punish.

We have an obligation to learn skills of leadership. Democracy requires that we become effective leaders.

We can no longer force proper behavior; we can only stimulate appropriate behavior.

In applying logical consequences, we should not remind, threaten, coax or talk too much.

We should remember that if logical consequences are used as a threat or imposed in anger, they become punishment.

We should avoid using logical consequences as disguised punishment. Many teachers and parents misuse logical consequences. They fool themselves and/or the children by replacing the word "punishment" with a nicer name. Unless the relationship between the misdeed and the consequence is congruent with the logic of community living and social interest, and is freely accepted by the child as reasonable, regardless of what it is called, it remains "punishment" and should not be used.

Remember that "time out" is usually considered as punishment by the child.

One of us, E. Ferguson, has asked hundreds of university students whether they had experienced "time out" as children. Most of them had, and almost all of them indicated that they interpreted it as punishment.

There is not always a natural consequence or a logical consequence for every situation. However, when adults tend to think in these terms, their own creativity will increase, and appropriate means may more often be found. Ask yourself, "What would happen if I didn't interfere?"

Logical consequences are an effective corrective procedure for children displaying Goal 1 behavior. For Goals 2 and 3, only natural consequences should be used. With Goal 4 behavior, do not use either.

Use of Logical Consequences	Use of Punishment
A learning process	A judicial proceeding
Adult plays the role of an educator	Adult plays the role of policeman, judge and jailer
Adult is understanding, empathetic	Adult is usually angry
Adult is interested in the situation and its outcome	Adult is interested in retaliation
Adult tries to be objective, with little emotional involvement	Adult often is subjective, with considerable emotional involvement
Expresses the reality of the social order, not of the person	Expresses the power of a personal authority
Has consequences intrinsically related to misbehavior	Has an arbitrary connection between the misbehavior and its consequences
Has no element of moral judgment	Inevitably involves some moral judgment
Is concerned with what will happen now	Is concerned with the past
Respects the child	Belittles or demeans the child
Distinguishes between the *deed* and the *doer*	Denotes sin
Child is accepted, although her behavior is not	Implies that the child has no value
Is firm but fair	Is often unfair
Voice is calm and friendly	Voice is loud and angry
Is appropriate in a democratic setting	Is *not* appropriate in a democratic setting

Many of the great philosophers and educators believed that punishment was useless for improving human behavior. Much of modern scientific research has shown that punishment at best suppresses behavior temporarily. Moreover, punishment very often brings about unwanted and disturbing behavior that is *far worse* than the behavior originally shown, which had led to the punishment in the first place. By using logical and natural consequences instead of punishment, the teacher allows reality to replace the authority of the adult. Reality guides us as adults. Why should it not do so for children? We as adults know that if we spend all our money today, we'll have none left tomorrow. We learned from our past recklessness.

Our children gain in wisdom when we help them with kindness to learn reality by applying the methods of natural consequences rather than punishments for misdeeds.

It is not easy to separate logical or natural consequences from punishment. Often the difference is evident in the teacher's tone of voice, and it invariably is different in the attitude toward the child. If the teacher says, "We will see what happens," to prepare the child for the natural consequences, this may reflect a kind of warning of how reality will play out, or it can reflect a threat. These words said in a friendly way can be seen as helpful and when said angrily are understood as a threat that implies punishment. Logical and natural consequences permit children to decide what they can and want to do about the situation.

What does a teacher often do when he is confronted with a noisy class? He adds his noise to that of the pupils. Instead, he could soften his voice or stop talking altogether. The children will see to it that the class will be quiet. It is essential that the teacher acts like a bystander, helping a child to respond to the demands of the situation rather than to the teacher's personal demands. As soon as the teacher gets upset, he becomes personally involved and turns the best consequence into a futile punitive act.

Here is an example of resolving a problem without fighting or losing face:

A kindergarten child always refused to come into the classroom unless coaxed. One day the teacher decided not to give her special attention but gave her the choice to stay out or come in. When the child saw that the first period was play and fun, she decided to join in. After that she entered the classroom each day by herself.

If a child is not listening in a reading lesson, the logical consequence would be to let her miss her turn for oral reading. Most children like to read aloud because it gives them the opportunity for center stage. This consequence will help train the child to become more careful and attentive.

If a whole class of young children is inattentive, the teacher can go to the back of the room and work at his desk. He may say, "Children, when you are ready you can ask me to teach you." It is surprising how often the class will elect a spokesperson to appeal to the teacher. This is less effective with older children and not advisable unless the class has had some democratic training.

A little girl misbehaved by continually falling off her tipped chair. The teacher removed the chair, without saying a word, and she had to stand. By the quiet action he avoided the power conflict. He impressed the child. If he had scolded her, the other pupils may have followed her example and she would have repeated it. Silent action by a teacher is always more effective than words.

A teacher cannot apply consequences when he is angry or upset. Consequences must be a logical or natural outcome of a series of events. An imaginative teacher can think of many different logical consequences that will be effective in promoting cooperative rather than competitive behavior. Teaching a class in a democratic atmosphere is always a pleasure.

Chapter Ten

Conflict Solving and How to Deal with Tyrants

Essential to a democratic classroom is a combination of firmness and kindness expressed in the teacher's attitude....Firmness implies self-respect; kindness implies respect for others....We can resolve our conflicts without either fighting or yielding, by both respecting others and respecting ourselves.

—**R. Dreikurs, B.B. Grunwald & F.C. Pepper,** *Maintaining Sanity in the Classroom,* **2nd ed.**

A five-year-old boy shouted, "Ms. Abrams, who's the boss around here—you or me?" This may be dismissed as a cute remark, but let's look at what is really happening. Since children have been exposed to all kinds of media they are demanding their rights, like any other minority group. No longer does the child consider himself inferior and the adult superior. We as teachers must recognize that each child is a unique, dignified human being and have respect for him at all times. Then a feeling of mutual trust can be established. And only in such a situation are teachers able to be really effective in their relationships with students.

By the time a child is six or seven years old, he has an expansive awareness of the world from constant exposure to mass media, the prime contributors being TV, videos/DVDs and the Internet. We must remember that although a child is an excellent observer, he is a very poor interpreter and needs someone to put his observations in proper perspective.

This involves empathy, listening to the child, trying to understand and helping him by showing him the decision-making process. If this is not done, these young children become "little tyrants" and eventually grow into very big tyrants who dominate and humiliate their wives, husbands, children, co-workers and neighbors. Little tyrants tyrannize their parents, playmates, neighbors, group leaders, classmates and teachers. Many have this behavior pattern well established before they leave the playpen.

Since you are a democratic teacher you can recognize and deal with these children by applying some principles and skills of conflict-solving. "Neither fight nor give in" is *always* the best solution. Many teachers do not realize that anyone who fights with a child is bound to lose in the long run because the child is a smart manipulator, and the teacher is no match for him.

Most people in conflict situations think that they can make the other person change by using words, and teachers who want to force a child often fall into the same trap. Words are supposed to be a means of communication, but in a conflict situation the child is unwilling to listen and the words become weapons.

When a child is in a temper-tantrum, it is useless to talk to him. Waiting quietly until the temper is over, or quietly but firmly removing him, is far more effective. In fact, talking to him is the worst possible procedure because it is probably exactly what the child wants, and the teacher is simply falling for his mistaken goal.

Wherever people live, conflicts are inevitable because of differences of opinion, interests and goals. This is particularly true of the group life of a teacher with children in a classroom. In the past, conflicts were resolved by the person or group in power. The teacher represented this power and was able to exert her authority to make children behave. But in a democratic setting, nobody is willing to accept imposition and defeat. Today, children resist this kind of autocratic force. Teachers try to tyrannize children and children try to tyrannize teachers, and both suffer from the inability to get along with each other.

Actually, if you know how to deal with conflicts, you will find that teaching is really a rewarding and enjoyable profession. Here is a typical classroom problem:

Ricardo is refusing to do his work and is disturbing the class. What does the teacher usually do in this situation?

First, she protests and tells him how wrong he is, and then, because he is so stubborn, she wearily gives in. The correct solution is to do the exact opposite. If the tyrannical child demands and argues, first, you simply reply, "You may have a point." Second, you do whatever you think is right. He cannot continue acting the tyrant unless you agree to stay and fight with him. If you do stay to try and convince him to conform, you will only get yourself involved in a losing battle. Do not fall into the trap of thinking, "I must stay and resolve this problem because my personal status is at stake." The misbehaving child and the rest of the class will consider your actions appropriately sidestepping the conflict and not consider you a coward if you wisely avoid seeking a clear-cut victory. You will not lose dignity: the class will respect you as a wise diplomat who can resolve the major conflict by sidestepping a battle.

No one gains anything by fighting or giving in, but most of us when confronted by a tyrant, either adult or child, usually do fight and eventually give in. When the pupil is the tyrant, he will almost always be able to force the teacher to do what he wants. As teachers, we need to be aware of this fact of classroom life. A teacher who understands the four goals of misbehaving children will be more able to cope with a conflict situation and realize that the conflict may be instigated by the child but is perpetuated by actions and attitudes of the teacher.

In a democratic setting, nobody is willing to accept imposition and defeat: every victory is short-lived. The techniques by which conflicts can be resolved in a democratic setting were well established by Alfred Adler in the early decades of the 20th century but are still inadequately known today.[1]

Teachers have to learn to influence children rather than to coerce them. We can effectively use social influences in a democratic classroom by sociometric testing and by the use of group dynamics. Mutual respect is a prerequisite to solving conflict situations. The following are four principles that can help in producing harmony. They were formulated by Rudolf Dreikurs[2] as a basis for conflict-solving in a democratic setting, in the classroom or anywhere else where conflict exists.

1. Don't fight and don't give in. When you fight, you violate respect for the child. When you give in, you violate respect for yourself.

2. One must identify the nature of the conflict. The issue of the conflict is hardly ever the stated reason about which the disagreement exists; it is usually the issue of the teacher's personal involvement, concern with status, with winning or losing, with vanity, ambition or other personal goals.

   When the conflict between teacher and student occurs with children under ten years old, the goals of misbehavior are easier to define as previously described. With teenagers, it is more complicated because other goals, like excitement, dating and sex—all recognized and promoted by the peer group—are involved in the conflict. The goal of peer acceptance is a strong motivator. In adults the goals of profit, power and prestige are often active ingredients in any fight.

   A teacher who can understand and identify the underlying cause of the conflict is moving toward a peaceful and cooperative class.

3. Reach agreement on what you want to do. We always want the other one to change.

   The only one who can freely change is you. When you change, then the whole relationship is changed. Extricating yourself is the first step in changing the agreement between teacher and child.

When two people fight they have made an agreement to do so. In order to have a fight each person in the conflict communicates the desire to fight and then finds "cooperation" with the antagonist. Everything we do with other people, including fighting, involves mutual agreement and "cooperation."

Only when one stops and thinks, "What can I do about this hostile situation?" can the conflict be resolved. Thinking only of what the opponent should do leaves no room for understanding, and nothing can be changed.

One must reach a new agreement. Few people consider this possible in a conflict situation. Actually, whatever happens in a relationship is based on agreement, communication and full participation. If one changes one's own role, a new agreement is inevitable. One usually thinks only of what the opponent should do—instead of thinking what one could do oneself.

4. Let everybody in the conflict participate in the decision-making: As soon as the child learns to talk, we should listen to him—we need democratic leadership that neither fights nor gives in, but integrates.

Conflicts cannot be resolved without shared responsibility, without full participation in decision-making of all the participants in a conflict. Democracy does not mean that everybody can do as he pleases. It requires leadership to integrate and to win mutual consent.

In Chapter 12, you will find that during the weekly discussion period all the pupils take part in the decision-making process. This scheduled time for discussing problems eliminates most of the conflicts that happen from day to day. But when these conflicts between teacher and child do occur, remember the following points:

- Respect the other person.
- Don't fight; don't give in.

· Pinpoint the issue.

· Change the agreement.

When attempting to solve any conflict, we must realize that in order to change the attitude of our opponents, we must first change our own attitude toward them. The secret is, in changing ourselves, the change in them will automatically follow. Don't push; pull! If we step aside and leave space, our antagonist will have room to move over to our position.

In all human-relationship problems the key words are "mutual respect." Even a tyrant of the worst kind, old or young, deserves our respect by virtue of his mere humanity. Many tyrants, because they are so insecure, appreciate our respect very deeply.

Dr. F. J. C. Seymour, former Assistant General Secretary of the Alberta Teachers' Association, provided the following suggestions to help resolve arguments:

1. Don't lose your temper; you'll lose your point.

2. Remember, you are striving to win an *agreement*, not an *argument*.

3. Apologize when you're wrong, even on a minor matter.

4. Don't imply superior knowledge or power.

5. Acknowledge with grace the significance of the other's comment or statement of fact.

6. Know and admit the impact of your demands.

7. Remember that the ability to separate fact from opinion is the mark of a clear mind and reflects intellectual integrity.

8. Stay with your point: pursue your objective but don't devastate.

9. Don't quibble: say what you mean and mean what you say. If you want truth, give it.

10. Bargain in good faith. Your intellect will tell you when you are bargaining and your conscience will tell you whether you have good faith.

As long as we regard the tyrants in our schools as monsters, they will behave accordingly. On the other hand, if we respect them as human beings with an honest expression of equality, without giving in, then we are more likely to live with such tyrants peacefully and perhaps change their attitude to one of cooperation. This is especially true, the younger the child. Although young children can be destructive and tyrannical, with the ideas and methods in this book the teacher can learn to win these children's confidence, trust and cooperation.

NOTES

1. A. Adler, *Practice and Theory of Individual Psychology* (New York: Humanitas Press, 1927).

   A. Adler, *The Science of Living* (New York: Anchor Books, 1969; originally published in 1929).

   A. Adler, *What Life Should Mean to You* (New York: Putnam Capricorn Books, 1958; originally published in 1931).

2. R. Dreikurs, "*Technology of conflict resolution*," Journal of Individual Psychology 28 (1972): 203–206.

   R. Dreikurs, "Toward a technology of human relationship," *Journal of Individual Psychology* 28 (1972): 127–136.

Chapter Eleven

Is Your Class a Group?

*Do you regard your class as a mirror of your own person-
ality, feeling confident only when they obey and inadequate
when they disturb? Or do you really feel that you belong
to your class as a group member?*

—**R. Dreikurs**

It is unfortunate that we spend more time struggling against an
untrained child than we spend in training her to socialize in the life
of a group. In the previous chapters we have learned what makes a
child tick; now we will find out how a child ticks (in a group).

We suffer from a deep unrecognized prejudice toward children.
We fail to recognize their strengths or capacities. Most teachers
assume that they single-handedly have to teach and to correct a
given number of children in their class, be it large or small. But if
the teacher knows how to be a group leader, it should make little
difference whether there are 10, 30 or 50 children, because it is still
only one class.

We need special skills to utilize group dynamics and to create a
group atmosphere in which all students become willing and able to
learn, as one cohesive and cooperative group. This does not necessarily mean that the children are homogeneous in age or ability.

As we use various instructional methods and organizational plans for teaching specific lessons, we find it increasingly important to integrate the pupils, either as classes or for certain periods each day. In fact, if we don't make an effort towards this integration, we soon find that any class is split between those who are with us and those who are against us.

The Sociometric Test

A sociometric test can be useful to help the enthusiastic teacher understand and integrate subgroups in his class; to integrate the "isolate" (a withdrawn child or a child who has alienated the other children through misbehavior so that they do not wish to include her); and to improve the children's relationships and social interaction. The results of such a test can influence the seating plan in the classroom, the grouping of students for projects or enterprises, the formation of committees and the understanding of cliques and leaders.

Before giving the test, observe the following precautions:

1. Members of the group should know each other rather well.

2. The entire process should be completed as casually as possible.

3. Pupils must feel that the information will be treated with confidence.

4. Pupils must feel that the teacher is trying to help.

5. The word "test" should be avoided; its use may cause some pupils to give the "right" answers rather than the "correct" ones.

6. Clear questions must be asked.

7. Questions must apply to only one situation and the pupils must understand this.

8. Pupils must understand how the results are to be used.

9. The results should be used as soon as possible and the pupils should be aware that they are being used.

Bearing in mind that the purpose of the test is two-fold—diagnostic and as a basis for changes in relationships—the questions asked must be meaningful and well within the realms of reality for every student. The questions may be:

1. Name three pupils in the class that you would like to sit with.

    (a) If there is one person that you would prefer not to sit with, name that person. You may leave this question unanswered if that is your choice.

2. Name three pupils in the class that you enjoy playing with in the yard.

    (a) If there is one person that you would prefer not to play with, name that person. You may also leave this question unanswered.

3. In working on a group project name three people that you would like to work with.

    (a) If there is one person that you would prefer not to work with, name that person. You may leave this question unanswered.

From these six questions you will get sufficient information to see a clear picture of the group dynamics operating within the class. On the following page you will find a description of how to summarize this information graphically.

Sociometric Test Results

To summarize the data from a matrix and point them up more graphically, the target method is useful. To construct a target, draw four concentric circles as shown below.

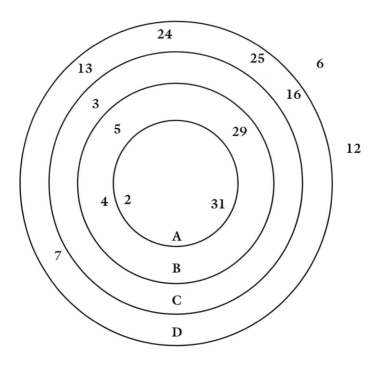

First, give each child a number. Then, in the circle in the center, A, the bull's eye, insert the number of pupils who receive more positive choices than would occur if the choices were evenly distributed among all the pupils. If each pupil is asked to choose three others she likes, an even distribution would give each pupil three votes. In this case, pupils who receive four or more positive choices, and no negative choices, are placed in the bull's eye.

In ring D, insert the numbers of those pupils who receive four or more negative choices or rejections, and one or no positive choices. In ring B, insert the numbers of those who are more liked than disliked, even though they are not chosen often. In ring C, insert the numbers of those who are more disliked than liked. Insert the numbers of the neglected students outside the target area.

You may be thinking, "Now that I have this information, what do I do with it?"

For group project work, it is more profitable to put compatible students together. They will contribute to a task with the least friction.

The isolates can be encouraged to join an extroverted group where they can experience new socialization skills or a buddy system that the teacher can set up with volunteers from the class. On the playground, the teacher can steer the isolate toward group games by giving her the class ball or another piece of sports equipment.

The seating plan of the classroom can be rearranged to accommodate the preferences of the pupils. Of course, if discipline problems do arise from friends talking together instead of working, you will need to change the seating plan again. But don't anticipate trouble; usually the pupils appreciate recognition of their request and cooperate as a sign of gratitude. They like to be near their friends and appreciate a teacher who shows this kind of understanding.

It is interesting to repeat the sociometric test procedure two or three times a year in order to find out what new relationships have been established and hopefully after some time to have no isolates at all. This is a realistic aim as a class moves towards cooperative cohesion.

Chapter Twelve

The Class Discussion Period

Children accept responsibility at a very early age if the adults give them a chance.

—**R. Dreikurs,** *Dreikurs Sayings*

We can teach responsibility only by giving the pupils opportunities to accept responsibilities themselves.

—**R. Dreikurs**

It is important to remember that any problem child is a problem for the whole class, and the solution to the problem grows most naturally out of the helpful involvement of all class members. If the teacher makes use of the cooperation of the pupils instead of exerting his own authority for behavior correction, there will be many advantages for all. The discouraged or misbehaving child will begin to feel she belongs to the group. This will reduce her discouragement and stimulate her to change her behavior. The class members will feel less frustrated about a miserable situation and will enjoy the opportunity to contribute to its improvement. They will learn to think positively about the discouraged child and become more tolerant human beings. Their prejudices will lessen. They will learn to express constructive ideas. They will feel not only that they are accepted by the group but they will also feel a sense of satisfaction that they are helping others to be accepted.

From the teacher's quiet but concerned action, the class members learn that there are methods of solving personality differences other than fighting. The teacher has extricated himself from a futile personal battle with the child. He maintains mutual respect and a pleasant relationship with all class members by not letting them choose to side with either the teacher or the disturber. The teacher's position is not threatened, and he can truly see social growth in the class. With this feeling of satisfaction he can leave the school each day relaxed and ready to enjoy his leisure time, without anxiety.

During the past two millennia, when political and religious hierarchies imposed decisions on most people of the world, democratic problem solving and human relations skills were not considered needed by either the rulers or the people who were ruled. Today children are raised in a democracy, and there is an implicit right and indeed a responsibility for all of us to express our opinions for the common good. Group discussions in the classroom are essential in this democratic setting. As a group leader, the teacher can learn important information about the children, their individual problems and their relationships with each other. The teacher can then guide the students in the continuous educational process.

The discussion period should not just happen as the need arises, but should be structured into the weekly timetable. It is essential that the pupils know that the lines of communication are open at a specified time *every* week. Even if there is little to discuss in a particular week, the opportunity is provided to the class. It is surprising how many problems that were daily occurrences will disappear once the discussion periods have begun. Consequently, the teacher can concentrate on teaching, without so many interruptions from disturbers or pupils with social problems in the classroom or in the schoolyard.

If there were no scheduled discussion periods, students would go to the teacher at any time that a problem arises. In contrast, when the pupils can expect their problems to be considered at the regularly scheduled discussion time, at in-between times they do not immediately go to the teacher for help whenever they encounter a problem. They will either wait patiently for a few days or solve the problem themselves (which of course is what we are training them to do). After waiting a few days, the original bad tempers will have subsided and a more rational approach is made possible during the presentation of the problem and discussion surrounding the solution.

Without class discussions, hostilities arise that can snowball into producing a miserable atmosphere for students and teacher alike. Group discussions provide the teacher with an opportunity to help the children understand themselves, and to change their concept of themselves and others, which will eventually change their attitudes from hostile to cooperative.

The Class Discussion Format

The following is a suggested format for the weekly class discussion. Teachers may choose slightly longer times, but a period of thirty minutes works well. Initially, the teacher is the chairperson, but after the students become familiar with the process and the role of the chairperson (which is to conduct the proceedings and disallow rudeness, insults, word fighting and slurs regarding gender, religion, ethnicity, race or color), the pupils themselves can take on the chairperson responsibility on a rotating basis. This gives the individual pupil an opportunity to experiment with her potential leadership qualities.

At the beginning of the period, five headings should be written on the blackboard:

1. Good things of the past week

2. Ways in which we can improve next week

3. Personal problems

4. Responsibilities

5. Future plans

Some teachers use a method that has each member of the class make one positive statement about her neighbor to the right before the discussion begins. The students and teacher sit in a circle and each individual makes one comment about her neighbor until the circle has been completed. Each statement is kept short and brief. The children in this way are trained to look for good qualities in each other or good actions taken by others. A less structured discussion then follows, which covers the above kinds of topics. This works well when the class is not very large.

Other teachers do not follow this method, but right from the beginning of the discussion they follow a pattern of covering the above five topics. As points are raised, mostly by the students, they are written down under the headings by either the teacher or a student, so that the discussion period can be summarized and quickly reviewed at the end of each session. Also, allow only five to six minutes to discuss topics under each heading in order to prevent wasting time by getting off-track. If discussions do get off-track, it is the chairperson's responsibility to bring them back on track.

The teacher should stress that the pupils concentrate on the positive and express only supportive suggestions. When negative comments are voiced, they should be dealt with only briefly and than re-formulated into a constructive way. The teacher has the opportunity in the classroom discussion to disclose the mistaken goals of students who the teacher believes need goal disclosure. If this is done according to the suggestions in Chapter 4, "How Does a Child Grow?" the pupils will not feel put down and the whole class will learn about the four mistaken goals. This will help other children change their own behavior as a result of their new understanding.

Any group discussion that involves goal disclosure is as valuable for all group members as it is for the actual pupil being counseled. Many class members will have feelings of discouragement. These are founded on their own personal opinions. When they hear that other pupils have similar feelings, they will feel more confident about themselves. They will also learn that self-perception is not always accurate, and that other people don't necessarily have the same low opinion of us as we may have of ourselves.

There is no doubt that class discussions are invaluable to the socialization process, to help all children feel comfortable about themselves and to aid them in the difficult process of growing up.

The Dynamics of Group Discussions

Group discussions serve three purposes. The first is that everybody has to learn to listen. At the present time, nobody knows how the others feel. How much do teachers actually "listen" to children? On the other side, while children do listen (we hope) to the teacher, how much do they know about how he is really feeling? The group discussion allows the children and the teacher to know how others feel and what they think.

The second function of the discussion periods is to help children to understand themselves and each other. To do so, the teacher must be acquainted with a psychological understanding of the children, particularly of their goals. Class group discussions are centered around the goals of the child's behavior. This eliminates fault-finding, preaching and sitting in judgment, which are all contrary to the spirit of free discussion.

In the beginning, the teacher may cite the problem a child is experiencing without mentioning a name. Soon the pupil will volunteer to identify herself. Children are very interested in such discussion and soon begin to ask personal and pertinent questions. They volunteer information about how they have tried to gain attention, show their power, get even or give up in discouragement, although prior to the discussion they might not have realized what they were doing.

The third goal of class discussions is to stimulate each child to help another. It is no longer the teacher with his authority and superiority who "instructs"; the children assist each other in finding better responses to their problems. Thus, the discussion turns the class into a cohesive group. The children soon begin to feel how much they have in common. The spirit of competition is replaced by an atmosphere of mutual empathy and help. The weaker one, who previously was an object of scorn and contempt, now becomes a friend who needs support and assistance. The fortunate child who succeeds socially and academically can no longer bask in the glory of her excellence, but realizes her responsibility for service and support to others.

The aim of group discussion is always for building trust, cooperation and social interest. The aim is never for belittling, demeaning, or humiliating and punishing. When children start to "gang up" on a member of the group, the chairperson and other members of the group immediately halt this with a reminder that group discussion is for *solving* problems, not creating them. The children from the beginning learn from the teacher that "ganging up" is a way of creating more difficulties, not a way for helping. The "ground rules" that the children learn from the initial class discussion is that the aim is to help the group and the individuals, to build understanding and mutual respect, to increase co-operation, and for the members of the class to enjoy each other and their learning experiences.

In this way group discussions are very effective in changing behavior and attitudes. The group can help heal hurts and problems in ways that are not otherwise possible. Something happens in a group discussion that has a more potent effect on behavior than a teacher's lecture or personal help could ever achieve. Children learn more from each other than from what the teacher says. In many cases, particularly in dealing with older and more defiant students, group discussion is the only way they can be reached. Classroom discussions can even counteract delinquent tendencies.

The Keys to Holding Successful Class Discussions

What is considered to be the generation gap is a "values" gap. It can be bridged through class discussion. Many young people believe that adults cannot understand them and cannot be their friend, that they cannot accept or understand the young person's values and beliefs.

Values can be changed in a group, because every group is a value-forming agent. In this way, with the help of the rest of the students, the teacher can bring up for discussion the ideas and values of every member of the class for scrutiny and reconsideration. However, this can be done only if the teacher refrains from lecturing and holding a narrow viewpoint and also preventing the children from moralizing and putting down their peers.

For a successful discussion period, the teacher, as the group leader, establishes with empathy and breadth of vision, a congenial group atmosphere. Only one person talks at a time and all the others learn to listen actively. No disturbance or rude interruption is acceptable or tolerated. The discussion stops until order is re-established. It may be advisable to appoint a secretary to take the "minutes" of the discussion period and read them at the start of the next class discussion.

You, as the teacher, cannot integrate the class or win the support of the students unless you sit down with them at least once a week and talk things over. It is amazing what we can learn when we really listen to the students. We, as adults, are always inclined to overestimate our own reactions and what happens to ourselves, and neglect seeing what we are doing to others, particularly to our pupils.

So our first step is to listen to each other; the second is to help each other to understand what each thinks—and feels. This produces an atmosphere of mutual help. The sharing of thoughts and feelings has strong therapeutic value, not only in the contents of the discussion, but also in the pure freedom to talk openly without fear of ridicule. Children have a need to talk and seldom have an opportunity to discuss things that really matter to them.

Discussion is a sharing medium. The child who cannot share herself is usually a lonely child, one who is constantly on guard and afraid of being hurt. She feels threatened by the idea of giving of herself and cannot participate in a discussion on a give-and-take basis. The introverted child will withdraw from participation in group discussion, as she withdraws from almost all participation.

You may ask, "What is the value of group discussion when the individual children have such problems?" But, this is the secret—they have an opportunity to solve their problems in a nonjudgmental, empathetic group setting. They participate by being in the group discussion even if they say nothing. They learn from others and have that important sense of belonging.

In a group discussion, the immediate focus is on the problem, as it affects everyone, and not on the individual child. Class discussions must start as soon as the teacher becomes acquainted with his class, perhaps even on the first day of school in the new academic year. Such a discussion may concern the decorating of the classroom, planning the activities for the first week, establishing class rules, etc. Both you and the pupils may propose rules that are necessary to maintain order. They should be reasonable and understandable. After these rules have been accepted by consensus, they should be posted on a blackboard or bulletin board where all pupils can quickly refer to them. Because the rules are logical, the pupils will want to abide by them not merely to please an authority, but because it is the proper thing to do.

"But," you may ask, "what happens if a pupil disobeys one of the rules?"

The consequences of violating a rule may be decided by the teacher immediately or by the class at the next discussion period. The important principle to be followed is that the child learns by her own experience that the infringement of order is not beneficial to her.

Here is an example. The class has agreed that playing ball near the school windows is not allowed because a window could get broken. Shannon disobeys the rule and while playing ball breaks a window. The class decides during the discussion period that Shannon should forfeit part of her allowance over a period of time to pay for the replacement window. In this way, Shannon learns to respect property and to understand why she should not play near the windows.

Studies have shown that regularly scheduled class discussions lead to fewer incidents of vandalism in a school, and pupils who had previously displayed delinquent behavior became cooperative when they felt they were integrated into the group.

Group discussions provide a sense of belonging and a sense of trust that are vital for any class. Even children as young as five-year-olds in kindergarten have participated in class discussions and found them to be very enjoyable. Older children rely on this method once they have experienced it, and value it as a highly effective democratic process for sharing and problem solving.

Here are some comments from children in Grades 3 and 4 concerning their classroom discussion periods:

"It's nice to share our problems."

"It's a good feeling to be understood and helped."

"It's nice to be able to help others."

"Thirty heads are better than one."

"We feel more confident now."

"We like to know what to expect in the next week; it gives us a feeling of security."

"We have learned to solve our own problems."

"We like to plan extra activities (creativity)."

"It's fun to know how we are all trying to improve in the next week."

Table 12.1: Discussion guide for a large group (10 or more) that helps to promote democratic principles

Good things in the past week	Ways in which we can improve next week	Problems	Responsibilities	Future plans
Strengths	Treat improvement as group improvement rather than singling out individuals	Responsibility for solving problems lies with the group	Jobs to be done in the classroom to be shared and rotated	Build on positives: "What can we do to make our class (group, etc.) more pleasant?"
Verbalize the events that were satisfying, fun, exciting, proof of class accomplishment	Decision making	"What can we do about it" is a group-thinking action	Help to promote cooperation and team spirit	May include plans for fun activities
	Participation	Use a Suggestion box		Suggestions are made by individuals
	Consensus	Look what I can do for you rather than what you should do		The group will decide if plans are realistic or not
	Avoid voting because the losers will refuse to cooperate with plans for improvement			

Discussion period

30 minutes duration is recommended

Teacher is chairperson first time, then rotate

Important points

Don't waste air time—remember others want a turn

Contracts to be kept for one week

Emergency meetings only in very unusual situations

Democratic rules

Raise your hand.

One person speaks at a time.

Be responsible.

Use mutual respect.

Be positive.

Don't clam up.

State your opinion clearly.

Think together.

Use logical decision-making skills.

Solve problems with cooperation and by meeting the needs of the situation.

Creative tasks or tasks for mischief makers

Chairperson of the week

Timer

Recorder

Committee Chairperson

Chapter Thirteen

Typical Problems in the Classroom and Their Solutions

It seems that one purpose of education is to turn clever children as rapidly as possible into stupid adults.

—R. Dreikurs

This sentiment has been expressed by many eminent educators. But if modern teachers were to use the two techniques of diagnosing the four goals and integrating the class, we would soon reverse the above statement and help most children to become cooperative adults.

Here are some examples of typical misbehavior by children at elementary school. See if you can ascertain the child's mistaken goal: 1) Attention; 2) Power; 3) Revenge or 4) Display of Inadequacy. Remember that the child is not consciously aware of his goal. The child only becomes aware of it, and shows awareness by means of the "recognition reflex," when you correctly identify the goal in the way that this book is describing. When diagnosing the child's immediate mistaken goal, it is advisable to consider the following:

1. What did the description of the behavior really say about the child's purpose?

2. What was the teacher's feeling response to the inappropriate behavior?

3. What did the teacher do that possibly reinforced the mistaken goal?

4. What was the child's next move?

Example One

Angelo has dropped his pencil deliberately for the fifth time this morning. This has occurred many times over the past few weeks. The teacher feels annoyed. She has repeatedly reminded Angelo to be more careful and has often talked and scolded about the disturbances. Now the teacher feels that Angelo occupies too much of her time.

The mistaken goal is Goal 1—Attention. After the teacher has confirmed her suspicion by goal disclosure, and by seeing the recognition reflex, she can then apply the corrective procedure. She will ignore the pencil and paper dropping at this time but talk to Angelo about it later. She will compliment Angelo on cooperative behavior whenever possible; she will show an interest in him, but not at a time when Angelo demands or expects it, and gradually show that he is accepted and belongs to the class group. There will be no need for Angelo to exercise attention-getting behavior.

Example Two

Quincy adamantly refuses to finish his schoolwork. He is sullen and defiant, and prone to taunting other students. After the principal met with him to discuss his behavior, he threw a brick through a classroom window. When Quincy plays ball with the other boys, and his team is losing, he always complains and calls his opponents cheaters. The teacher has let the principal know she would like him removed from her class. She feels hurt and outraged by Quincy's behavior. She even dislikes him and wonders how he can be so mean.

You've guessed it. The mistaken goal is Goal 3—Revenge. After confronting Quincy with the goal of his misbehavior, and establishing that the goal is revenge, the teacher begins her plan of action. Even though she feels like telling him how hurt she is, she avoids the slightest indication. She decided not to punish him or shout at him again. She does unexpected things that please and surprise him. She encourages the group to like and support him. At the class discussion she asks for a volunteer to be his helpful buddy and friend. Within a short time she finds that Quincy asks for help with his work and is less distracted. He is soon focusing and concentrating much better.

Example Three

Alex has just launched a paperclip across the room using an elastic band as a sling-shot. His teacher has asked him to write an assignment on wolves, but as usual he is stubbornly refusing to follow instructions. Alex is in a particularly bad temper this day, and has argued constantly with his classmates and has done no work in any lesson. The teacher feels defeated and thinks, "He can't do this to me." At that moment another paperclip whizzes by her ear. She feels her authority and leadership are being threatened. She yells, "Alex, I will not tolerate this behavior. It stops now!"

No doubt you discovered the goal at the beginning of Alex's story. He is a typical "power drunk" child as described in Goal 2. When the teacher diagnoses Alex's goal, she will admit defeat inwardly or openly, or both. She will recognize Alex's power and give him opportunities to use it constructively. At all costs, she will avoid a power struggle with Alex and extricate herself from any conflict. She will show respect for Alex—even for the fact that he seems to have more power in the classroom than she has. She will not fight with him as Alex wants her to do—that would mean giving in to his provocation. By remaining kind and firm, she can lead him to find his place through better alternatives.

Example Four

Trish has become withdrawn and spends most of her school day staring blankly out of the window. She feels hopeless and acts "stupid." She appears to have an inferiority complex and rarely participates; when she does, it is short-lived. She might make an effort to do something, but the slightest challenge will make her give up. She seems to be saying subconsciously, "Leave me alone, you can't do anything with me." As Trish sits slumped at her desk, the teacher passes by and assesses the situation. The teacher feels helpless and throws up his hands, thinking, "I don't know what to do with you; I give up."

After confirming that this misbehavior is rooted in Goal 4—display of inadequacy—the teacher begins a strenuous encouragement program. He makes Trish feel worthwhile when she tries, and he encourages the child, particularly when Trish has made a mistake. The teacher uses a constructive approach and enlists the class's cooperation with pupil helpers. The aim of all the class is to show Trish that they have faith in her abilities to cope and meet the needs of the situation. Often the members of the class can exert a strong encouraging influence by showing their pleasure when the child shows an improvement, however slight it may be.

Chapter Fourteen

The Do's and Don'ts of Discipline

Knowing what not to do is a great help in determining what should be done.

—**R. Dreikurs,** *Dreikurs Sayings*

What can a teacher do for having the kind of classroom order that the teacher and the students both find satisfactory? Is this possible? It is if discipline and order are used as a cooperative enterprise, with understanding by both the teacher and the students and with their developing team spirit. In order to achieve this end, the teacher must know what not to do as well as what to do in a given situation. The following eight points are common approaches but produce negative results.

1. A preoccupation with one's authority may provoke rather than stifle defiance and resistance to discipline. Teachers should focus on their tasks and not be concerned with their own prestige.

2. Refrain from nagging and scolding, as it may fortify the child's mistaken concept of how to get attention.

3. Do not ask a child to promise anything. Most children will promise to change in order to get out of an uncomfortable situation. It is a sheer waste of time.

4. Do not give rewards for good behavior. This child may then work only in order to get a reward and stop as soon as this has been achieved. What's more, rewards will only

strengthen the student's belief that every courteous action or contribution should be met with a reward.

5. Refrain from finding fault with the child. It may hurt the student's self-esteem and be discouraging.

6. Avoid double standards, one for the teacher and another for the student. In a democratic atmosphere, everybody must have equal rights. This includes the chewing of gum, swearing, tardiness, unnecessary visiting and talking with members of the staff in class when the children are working, checking papers or doing any kind of work that prevents the teacher from looking at the child when talking to him.

7. Do not use threats as a method to discipline the child. Although some children may become intimidated and conform for the moment, it has no lasting value since it does not change their basic attitudes.

8. Do not be vindictive; it stirs up resentment and unfriendly feelings.

Let us now consider some of the effective measures that a teacher can use in the disciplinary procedure.

1. Because problem behavior is usually closely related to the child's faulty evaluation of his social position and how he must behave in order to have a place in the class group, the teacher's first concern must be to understand the purpose of this behavior. (See Chapters 5 and 14.) Only then will the teacher be in a position to plan more effectively for this child.

2. Give clear-cut directions for the expected action of the child. Wait until you have the attention of all class members before you proceed in giving directions.

3. Be more concerned with the future behavior of the child than with the one he exhibited in the past. Refrain from reminding the child about past actions.

4. As soon as a child misbehaves and tends to threaten the general atmosphere in the class, give him the choice either to remain seated without disturbing others, or leave the classroom. (This requires that arrangements are in place, which have been agreed to with the child and principal, regarding where the child should go.)

5. Build on the positive and minimize the negative. There is much good in every child, but if you look only for academic achievement you may never find the many fine qualities the child has.

6. Try to establish a relationship with the child built on trust and mutual respect.

7. Discuss the child's problem at a time when neither of you is emotionally charged, preferably in the regular class discussions.

8. Use natural and logical consequences instead of traditional punishment. The consequences must bear direct relationship to the behavior and must be understood by the child.

9. Be consistent in your decisions. Do not change decisions arbitrarily to suit a given your purpose at a given moment. Inconsistency confuses the child about what is expected of him at a certain procedure.

10. See behavior in its proper perspective. In this way you will avoid making a serious issue out of trivial incidents.

11. Establish cooperative planning for future task goals and the solution of problems.

12. Let children assume greater responsibility for their own behavior and learning. They cannot learn this unless we plan for such learning. Responsibility is taught by giving responsibility. Be prepared for children to act up at first. Such training takes time.

13. Use the class community to express disapproval quietly when a child behaves in an antisocial manner.

14. Treat the child with mutual respect.

15. Combine kindness with firmness. The child must always sense that you are a friend, but that you would not accept certain kinds of behavior.

16. At all times distinguish between the deed and the doer. This permits respect for the child, even when he does something wrong.

17. Guide the individual to assume independence and to assure his own self-direction.

18. Set the limits from the beginning, but work toward mutual understanding, a sense of responsibility and consideration for others.

19. Admit your mistakes—the children will respect your honesty. Nothing is as pathetic as a defeated authoritarian who does not want to admit defeat.

20. Mean what you say, but keep your demands simple, and see that they are carried out.

21. Children look to you for help and guidance. Give them this security but make cooperation and eventual self-control the goal.

22. Keep in mind your long-term goal: an independent responsible adult.

23. Children need direction and guidance until they can learn to direct themselves.

24. Close an incident quickly and revive good spirits. Let children know that mistakes are corrected and then forgotten.

25. Commend a child when his behavior in a situation shows improvement.

26. Work cooperatively with the children to develop a procedure for dealing with infractions of the rules.

27. "Do unto others as you would have them do unto you."

Chapter Fifteen

Classroom Experiences

*When we deal with a child, even the most difficult one,
we must have faith in that child. Pessimism gains
nothing; optimism is the only way to improve and
change behavior in others.*

—R. Dreikurs

This book is written in an informal way in order that it may help not only the individual dedicated to the career of teaching in schools, but also the person who thinks of teaching as a temporary vocation, for example, Brownie and Cub leaders, church group leaders, camp counselors, team coaches, etc. The following are the personal experiences of Pearl Cassel selected from among more than four decades of teaching elementary school children.

Jermyn, aged 11, often displayed Goal 2 (Power) and Goal 3 (Revenge) behavior. He was repeatedly late returning to the classroom after recess. One day I explained to the class that immediately after recess we'd be making a filmstrip. We were all very excited about this and planned the sequence of the story around Theseus and the Minotaur, with printing and drawings.

The children returned after recess and I gave them detailed instructions regarding size and dimensions. Jermyn returned to class after I had given the instructions. He saw that his classmates were working. After taking his seat, he asked, "Can I do what they are doing?" I replied, "Yes, you may." He looked at the work that the other children were doing, but they did not explain to him the importance of dimensions. He spent a full hour busily drawing and printing. At the end of the lesson, the pupils were displaying their work for evaluation.

When Jermyn held up his work, a classmate said, "We can't use that for our filmstrip because it is the wrong dimensions for the camera. " Jermyn said, "Nobody said anything to me about dimensions." Another classmate said, "The teacher told us, right after recess, and you weren't here."

Jermyn was very upset. His was the only piece of work that was not photographed. When he left school for the day, he took his work with him. After that day, he was never late returning from recess.

The logical consequence taught him far more effectively than any punishment would have. He learned without receiving special attention from the teacher or fighting in a power struggle. The result of this learning was a permanent change in behavior.

The following story is of a nine-year-old boy with severe spelling difficulties (and, as usual with problem spellers, he had little respect for order). Tim was withdrawn, deeply discouraged, in Goal 4, and showing continuous displays of inadequacy. He would even say, "Don't mark my work because I know it is all wrong."

A class project was started to improve the general standards of spelling, and the pupils worked in five separate groups. The word lists were compiled on Mondays, studied by the students during the week in various ways, and then the students were tested on the Fridays.

During a weekly discussion period, Tim's group complained that he was getting so many words incorrect that he was spoiling the group's improvement chart. They even wanted to evict him from their group. I asked then what they had done to help Tim. They replied, "Nothing." I then said, "What could we do to help him?" They suggested that some of them could help him after class in the afternoons. I asked Tim if he would like them to help him at this time. He appeared delighted.

On the next Monday, Tim's group set up a schedule for the next four days. Each afternoon a different volunteer played spelling games with him for ten minutes. On the following Friday he spelled his words perfectly. He was completely surprised and overjoyed. His group enthusiastically congratulated him. This procedure was repeated for three more weeks with a decreasing number of help periods until finally he managed to study his word list himself with satisfactory results.

The next example is a situation that was first mentioned at a class discussion. It was wintertime and one pupil made the following statement: "Our room looks a mess because there are always so many coats, hats and mitts lying on the floor at the back of the room, even though there're lots of coat hangers."

Another child said, "If anything is on the floor, it should either be put in the garbage can or taken to the 'lost and found' box." Another child suggested the idea that any clothing on the floor should automatically go to the "lost and found." It was agreed by consensus that this should immediately take effect. (It is important for the teacher to seek consensus, so that all children feel an equal share in the decision, and not to settle class decisions by a majority vote.)

The next morning there were about fifteen coats and hats lying on the floor. I said nothing but one of the children picked up an armful of clothes and asked his friend to help him. They both struggled to the box with all this clothing.

At recess there were fifteen children rummaging through the "lost and found" box for clothing. They missed most of their playtime. On the next day there were seven coats on the floor, and the following morning there were only three. Within a week we had eliminated the whole problem of clothing on the floor. The suggestion had come from the group, and the problem was solved by the group without any suggestion from me. This was truly group awareness in action.

At a later discussion period a pupil raised the point that two boys, Ray and Manuel, were spoiling their gymnastics lesson. I asked Ray and Manuel if this was true. They admitted it. After considerable discussion it was suggested by a class member that, at the beginning of the gymnastics lesson, Ray and Manuel would be allowed to demonstrate certain movements and somersaults of their choice, and the class would follow, and repeat these activities. This was agreed by consensus and the class cooperated in the next gymnastic lesson. After that there were no more disturbances from Ray or Manuel.

Problems and Solutions

Following are some more typical problems and their solutions. Try to solve the problem before you read the answer. Look for the clues: the description of the child's behavior; the actions of the teacher; and the words used to express the teacher's feelings. Annoyance indicates Goal 1; defeat, Goal 2; outrage, Goal 3; and helplessness, Goal 4. After referring to Tables 5.1 and 5.2 in Chapter 5, "Identifying and Correcting the Four Mistaken Goals," choose the corrective procedures the teacher might use.

Problem One

David is sitting, occasionally glancing around, and doing his mathematics as slowly as possible. He writes three numerals and rubs out two. He tries to write them better. Finally, after fifteen minutes he is satisfied so gives his attention to the second simple question. Meanwhile the teacher has been moving about the room helping others and reminding David to "hurry up." The teacher keeps wondering how she is going to make David work faster.

David is discouraged, has a poor self-image and is probably overly ambitious. The teacher has fallen for David's mistaken goal of attention-getting (Goal 1) by constantly reminding him to hurry. The teacher has taken his responsibility on herself and has made

David's problem *her* problem. David feels that he has a place in the class only when his work is perfect. He feels worthwhile only when he is on top. After confronting him with the four goals, and establishing that he is in fact seeking Goal 1, the teacher should do the following things to help David. She should encourage him not to be afraid to make mistakes and give him assurance that he is accepted as he is. She needs to assure him that he does not have to be perfect to be worthwhile. She should give him lots of attention, but only at times when he does not demand or expect it, and help him with work that he truly does not understand. She should refrain in class from reminding him to hurry up, but instead help him to make task goals for himself regarding his assignments and then leave him alone to complete them.

Problem Two

Maria puts up her hand and tells the teacher she doesn't know what to do. The exasperated teacher looks at Maria and asks if she was listening to the instructions. The teacher is annoyed at Maria and his voice indicates it. Maria has made a habit of not knowing what to do, and the teacher often reminds her of this in front of the class.

Maria is in Goal 1—destructive attention-getting—and the teacher is reinforcing Maria's mistaken goal. The clue to the child's misbehavior as being a function of Goal 1 is the teacher's reaction—his own annoyance. Instead of encouraging Maria to be responsible for herself, he further discourages Maria by embarrassing her. Then Maria feels obliged to live *down* to the teacher's expectations.

After querying Maria regarding the four goals to confirm that Maria is bidding unduly for attention, the teacher can decide that he will no longer show annoyance. He will encourage Maria to listen but will not repeat the instructions. If Maria does not know what to do, she will be unable to finish the assignment in the required time. The logical consequence is for Maria to finish the work in her own time after school. She would then learn to listen in future.

Problem Three

Susan is playing with the doll's house in the kindergarten. Elsa has been waiting patiently for her turn. The teacher suggests that Elsa have a turn. Susan throws down the doll, kicks the dollhouse and then stomps on the teacher's foot. The teacher wonders why Susan is so mean. The clue to the mistaken goal on which Susan is operating is the teacher's reaction of thinking, "How can Susan be so mean?" Susan's mistaken goal is that of Goal 3. By throwing the doll, kicking the doll's house and stepping on the teacher's foot, she is demonstrating an active-destructive way of revengefully seeking her place. We must realize that all behaviors, whether good or bad, of children under ten are directed toward the adult in order to gain significance.

After Susan has calmed down, the teacher should confront her with the four goals to discover if it really is Goal 3. She will then encourage Susan to feel that she is liked, perhaps by enlisting a volunteer buddy from the class. She will acknowledge Susan and respond in a warm and friendly way when her behavior is acceptable and keep her silence when it is not. She will constantly try to give Susan the feeling of belonging and sharing with the other children. When the teacher believes that Susan can behave in a socially acceptable manner, it is likely that Susan will respond to that trust. The teacher remembers, "Catch a kid doing something good."

Problem Four

Alyssa is very quiet in the classroom and never participates in the discussion periods. She often forgets to hand in assignments and when given a test rarely gets past the first question. On the day when a field trip was planned for the class she stayed at home, although she was not ill. The teacher has tried many times to interest Alyssa in the school subjects, but has never seen enthusiasm for anything. The teacher doesn't know what to do with her.

Alyssa is passive and self-defeated. She wants to be left alone and acts as if she is inferior and incapable. Since the teacher feels helpless, and Alyssa's social interest is so poorly developed that she does not even want to go on a field trip, we might guess that her mistaken goal is Goal 4. By using goal disclosure the teacher could confirm this. Alyssa is deeply discouraged and is crying out for reassurance. At the weekly class discussion the teacher will give Alyssa opportunities to contribute and will encourage the other children to include her in their activities. As Alyssa's confidence in her social relationships grows, she will feel more capable to tackle her work. When she feels that she really belongs, she will likely hand in the assignments.

Problem Five

Paul constantly argues with the teacher. In every science or history lesson he interrupts, saying that the teacher is wrong. When the class is asked to read the textbook, he tells jokes to the other students to distract them. Most of the teacher's lessons are spoiled by Paul. Whatever the teacher asks him to do, he does the opposite. The teacher feels exasperated and often thinks, "Who is running this class—is he or am I?"

Paul is a typical power-drunk boy who feels he has to control and challenge leadership in order to belong. By arguing, distracting and showing defiance, he opposes the teacher. The teacher feels threatened in her role and is continually in a power conflict with the boy who functions with Goal 2. After the teacher queries Paul for goal disclosure to find out if her guess is right, she can help Paul by giving him important and "powerful" things to do in the class that are acceptable and contribute to the class. She will not compete with him, but enlist his cooperation as an ally. When he argues, she will extricate herself from the conflict by remaining calm and saying nothing. At times she can publicly agree with him even when he is disturbing the class by telling him in an unemotional tone, "You have a point." By the teacher showing respect for

Paul, he will learn that he does not have to challenge in order to be part of the class. At the weekly class discussion period Paul can interact with his classmates less aggressively and gradually contribute positively.

Problem Six

Blake walks into the history class, looks around, sits down and starts to play with his pen. As the lesson proceeds, it is obvious to the teacher that Blake is taking no part in the lesson. He spends most of his time gazing out of the window. After the assignment is given the teacher walks around and notices that Blake has made no attempt even to start the assignment. The teacher tells Blake he will have to come back after school if he doesn't finish the assignment in class. Blake shrugs his shoulders and tells her that every other teacher wants him to stay as well. The teacher feels helpless and doesn't know what to do.

Blake's behavior of being an observer, rather than a participator, in the class is a symptom of his feelings of inadequacy. The teacher's reaction of feeling helpless indicates that she has fallen for Blake's mistaken goal (Goal 4). Obviously threat of punishment has not changed Blake's direction. He has given up, does not even try and has become so discouraged that he inhibits his own ability to learn.

After clarifying with Blake his mistaken goals to confirm the suspicion of Goal 4 (display of inadequacy), the teacher embarks on an encouragement program. Perhaps she can influence other teachers who are also having trouble with Blake. If the work assignments are within Blake's capabilities, she may get another student to sit with him. She can decide to mark only his correct responses, and ignore the mistakes, in order to help Blake feel that he is making some progress. She can tell the class sincerely that Blake, who got four answers out of 50 correct, has improved 100 percent, because in the last lesson he got only two responses correct.

You Can Stop the Tears and Enjoy Cooperation

In these examples we learn that the class discussion period can be vitally important to the healthy growth of the class as a group, and an essential encouragement process for misbehaving, discouraged pupils. As teachers learn to talk less, act more and respect students as individuals with enormous potential, they can then teach in a cooperative atmosphere where students are willing to learn and discipline problems are minimal. When the pressure of conflict is relaxed, teachers' own potential can then be released and the creativity of the students can be expressed. Because learning and intelligence are creative processes, we must provide the optimum environment for this growth in our classrooms.

As you apply the principles that are explained in this book you will be a happier, healthier and more relaxed teacher. Children's tears and your tears will be left in the past. You will find joy in your profession by sharing the ecstasy of life experiences with children who are eager to discover, explore, and share their new-found understandings with you—their teacher, leader and friend.

Appendix A

Codes of Conduct

The following describes contemporary developments that have set standards for teachers and students.

In April 2000, the Ministry of Education released the "Ontario Schools Code of Conduct" as a first step in ensuring that Ontario has safe schools. The document sets clear and consistent standards of behavior that apply to all publicly funded schools across the province. The establishment of standards is intended to foster a learning environment that is characterized by respect and civility. Students, parents and teachers and other staff members all need to feel that Ontario schools are safe places in which students can learn and teachers can teach. Although the consequences for infraction set out in the provincial code of conduct apply to students who ignore the rules, everyone—not just students—will be expected to hold the same standards of behavior.

Legislation and Ministry Policy on Codes of Conduct

1. To ensure that all members of the school community, especially people in positions of authority, are treated with respect and dignity.

2. To promote responsible citizenship by encouraging appropriate participation in the civic life of the school community.

3. To maintain an environment where conflict and difference can be addressed in a manner characterized by respect and civility.

4. To encourage the use of non-violent means to resolve conflict.

In developing local standards of behavior the principal must take into consideration the views of the school council. In addition he, or she, should seek input from students, staff, parents or guardians, and members of the community; include procedures and timelines for review, in accordance with school board policy; develop a communications plan that outlines how these standards will be made clear to everyone, including parents and guardians whose first language is English or French.

A Typical "Senior School" Philosophy

All general conduct rules can be reduced to courteous and common sense behavior that shows respect for the rights and feelings of others. The Ontario "Code of Behaviour" applies to all school and school-related activities, curricular and co-curricular, both on and off school property, including all athletic events. A student who breaks any of the policies contained in the Code of Behaviour can expect appropriate consequences to result. These consequences can be of such nature as detentions, extra assignments, clean-up of school grounds, parental involvement and suspension. The services of the vice-principals and counselors are available to all students to assist in resolving difficulties and conflicts.

Appendix B

Suggested Further Reading

Barber, J., and J. Allan. *Managing Common Classroom Problems.* Toronto: University of Toronto Guidance Centre, 1986.

Cassel, P., and R. Corsini. *The Challenge of Adolescence.* Toronto: Crystal Cassel, 1998.

Cassel, P., and R. Corsini. *Coping with Teenagers in a Democracy.* Toronto: Lugus Productions, 1990.

Dinkmeyer, D., and R. Dreikurs. *Encouraging Children to Learn: The Encouragement Process.* Philadelphia: Brunner-Routledge, 2000.

Dreikurs, R., B. B. Grunwald, and F. Pepper. *Maintaining Sanity in the Classroom.* Philadelphia: Taylor and Francis, 1998.

Dreikurs, R., and V. Soltz. *Children: The Challenge.* New York: Penguin, 2003.

Ferguson, E. D. *Adlerian Theory: An Introduction.* Chicago: Adler School of Professional Psychology, 2002.

Grunwald, B. B., and H. McAbee. *Guiding the Family.* 2nd ed. Philadelphia: Taylor and Francis, 2000.

Index